BITE HARD

BITE HARD

Justin Chin

MANIC D PRESS
SAN FRANCISCO

To Morgan, Zack & Lisa

Grateful acknowledgments is made to the following publications in which some of these writings first appeared in slightly different forms:
5 A.M., Alchemy, Americas Review, Bamboo Ridge: The Hawaii Writers Quarterly, Beloit Poetry Journal, Blue Mesa Review, The Evergreen Chronicles, Oxygen, Plazm, Puerto Del Sol, Rites, Sonora Review, Shantih: Anthology of Chinese/Chinese-American Poetry, Dissident Song: A Contemporary Asian American Anthology, Premonitions: The Kaya Anthology of New Asian American Poetry, Eros in Boystown, and *Best Gay Erotica 1997.*

The author wishes to thank David Thomson, DeCat, Regie Cabico, Lois-Ann Yamanaka, Jennifer Joseph, and all the folks on the road who have given me a place to crash and an ear for endless hours of it all.

5 4 3

Library of Congress Cataloging-In-Publication Data

Chin, Justin, 1969-
  Bite hard / Justin Chin.
     p. cm.
  ISBN 0-916397-47-5 (pbk.)
     1. Asian American gays--Literary collections. 2. Gay men--United States--Literary collections. I. Title.
PS3553.H48973B5 1997
818'.5409--dc21   97-4716
                                                              CIP

CONTENTS

Lingual Guilts

Bitter   9

Communion, Said The Barfly   16

Fate   19

Risings   21

Flying the Red Eye   24

Positivity   25

Bestiality   26

The End   27

Pot   28

Night   29

Bangkok   31

Crabs From A Gun   32

The Ballad of Dependency   33

A History of Geography   35

Flesh/Wound   38

The Secret Life of Flowers   41

Sold

Sold   47

State   49

This Is Your Life   51

Tied   53

Bar Poem   55

Luck   57

The Bridegroom   58

Swoop   60

Bergamot   62

Hypothermia   63

Zoo Animals   65

Travelogue   67

The Only Living Man In The World   69

Nervous Days

Chinese Restaurant   73
Why He Had To Go   75
Buffed Fag   76
Back When I Knew Who I Was   77
Phone Sex   80
Lick My Butt   82
Itchy   85
Eurodisco   87
These Nervous Days   89
Smooch   91
Ex-Boyfriends Named Michael   93
Home   95
Tour   97

Pisser

Cocksucker's Blues   103
Pisser   106
Why A Boy   108
Postcard Angels   110
Chinese New Year   113
Refuging   116

Lingual Guilts

Bitter

Bitterness comes as revolution,
cyclic, a snake
biting its tail scales,
a dog nipping its tail hairs, bitter,
continuity achieved by subtlety,
perceptions played out,
questions followed by answers,
ask, answer, some days
you will know, others
you wake to nothing of the same,
the smell of washed grass,
I have this theory: the rain
each drop, big as bees, falls
with a velocity to bore into the ground,
tilling the grass smell out
of the air pockets in the earth,
the pine cones and the sea smell
saltiness washed clean with Absolut,
this is another country,
this is a different place,
the water tastes different
and the Indian money changer
with the stained dhoti and turban
smelling of coconut oils and incense,
sitting cross-legged at his pavement box store
respects you for your money,
and your whiteness stands out
like wine stains on the hotel sheets,
where I spilled a half bottle
as we wrestled, our naked bodies
pressed against the sweaty halfjest,
facing the expansiveness
of the night and the buzzing
traffic, plays
its points of red and yellow
against the window panes
while we lay watching the stars
quiver and descend to inches

before our eyes as strangers
start to sprout hair all over
their arms, faces, legs and slowly
turn into large orangutans driving taxicabs,
and the universe churns around us
like a ride at Disneyland,
disappearing into flat
unbroken scheme.
These were the lost years,
writing really bad poems,
arguing with border guards,
this Walkman is not new,
there's no tax anyway,
reading incomprehensible Beckett plays,
discussing Gide and Orton
tripping on dope bought from the bellboy,
cheap wine from the Japanese departmental store,
working on my tan,
trying to add inches to my arms,
listening to you detail your research
on crossculturalisms, here,
as we get off at the station
built to look like a mosque
with the grandeur of bright mosaic
tiles spiraling up dome structures
and intricately craved wood
panelings to hide the grime
and the weary travelers,
rudely shouting at everybody.
In the restroom, I squat
hovering over the hole in the floor
trying to work the uneasiness
out of my stomach as I hear scraping
of feet in the stall beside me,
under the partition, there are two pairs
of shoes, moving in a slow, frantic,
desperate dance, trying to carve
a small slice of validity, to find their heaven
in this hemisphere of spent contradictions,
in this two feet of shit-odored
space, they have found their judgment

and I leave them
to find a pay phone,
my father tells me that the sultana is dead,
the TV programmings have been replaced
with Koranic dirges and everybody
is expected to wear black armbands:
mandatory mourning will be checked on
by the police, so he wears an armband even
while playing all eighteen holes of golf,
to be Chinese here is a *bloody crime*,
he says and tells me to come home soon.
Clutching our tickets to the crosswise
third-class seats, we slouch backwards
towards the darkness, feeling
the close and warmth of our bodies
disentangle and the distance, marked
by the ashes of burning cane fields sticking
to our flesh, the attraction between two bodies
defined beyond gravity
grows heavy as the night falls,
and waving kampung children
accompanied by their elders and parents
give way to paddy fields and tobacco plantations,
lit by night lights and the glow
of the owner's small huts,
speed in front of our field of vision
hushing us to sleep, until
the feeling of urgency wakes me,
heart beating like slacks in a bicycle chain,
I find your body twitching ecstatically
while you rub yourself and metal shards
trickle out of your pants zipper
and turn rusty as I catch them
in my palm before they hit the floor,
the red dust etches itself into the
lines of my hands and the Nonya woman
sitting across the aisle, facing me,
takes my hands, spits into them,
the metal cuts into my hands
and I am left holding the remnants
of our sex, like an offering

to saints unknown, gods unbelieved,
searching for the spiritual
in the physicalness of your body,
dust weaves a maze into our bones,
femur holding suspended fragments
of torn secrecy, jealousy, bitter,
hip bone framing the ravishing, all
held in place with ligaments
fragile as pins and cobwebs,
straining to the lure of hunger,
as we make our way in the splash
of early morning sunlight, yellow
throwing long drawn out shadows
on the walls, through the first-class carriage,
through the recycled air-conditioned air,
smelling of sweating passengers, bleary-eyed
agog at the English-dubbed, the original
Cantonese captioned, kung fu movie
on the small TV screen, dangling
like bait from the ceiling,
to the dining car where
the overpriced cheese sandwiches melt
deliciously sticky and rancid.
The pull of the station brings us
to our destination,
as we set on the platform,
a swarm of brown-skinned boys, all
flashing their brightest Colgate smiles
want to take your backpack, help you
find a hotel, take you to lunch,
let you take them to dinner;
I am not an entity here,
I am competition in their minds,
more likely some cheap slut, a paid whore
who can be bested easily, they know that.
We find our regular boarding house
and the German expatriate,
a longtime resident, greets us and displays
the new boy he picked up in the park,
gave a good scrubbing to and dressed
in neatly pressed schoolboy outfits

for as long as the skinny wide-eyed
fawning boy wants to give handjobs.
The boy offers to do your laundry,
the English woman, a new resident,
invites us for a drink up on the roof
this evening, everybody seems glad
to see you again and the voices
flood into us like madness, pulling
us into the tenderness of untruth.
I invent space, poison, bitter,
snake bites, safety,
fester, if you boil roses
for twenty hours with a teaspoon
of fine sugar, stirring
clockwise, then steaming your face
in the saccharin fumes,
you will be loved, I invent
sweeping, mementos, maturity
and still, nothing
moves, stillness holds your tongue
and it breaks into thorns
sharp enough to pierce through
penitent flesh, wrapping itself
like a python squeezing the last
out of what's left of the moon
reflected on the river as the peddlers
calmly row their sampans laden
with tourist trinkets and vegetables
home; I know the temples
of gold and saffron
that burn incense and powders
on the tongue, deviled,
cutting sinners to jewels
washed in front of Buddhas
with smooth nipples and Egyptian eyes
that said *stay*
and you did.
Lying in the room, cast
a strange orange by the cellophane paper
over the windows, we laid plans,
mapping the fluidity of your life

and mine: I will go south,
to the East Coast to the sea, home
eventually, you will stay and try find
another boy: stranger angels
have beset us, and trains
are stories of sacraments
melting on the tongue, holy,
unspoken, blessed, and thoroughly
immaterial, totally bloodless,
the middleman calls,
there is no hardness
left, your body,
opaque, dense as familiarity,
leaves no stains, no inventions;
the German has found a new boy,
the train is delayed:
an elephant caused a derailment,
the platform is wheels, nothing
can hurt, I float in sea foam,
fine rain and bitter salt,
disenchanted, drawn to decency, shaping
pictures to memory that redefine
visions, transforming virginities,
pure, burning
in the smell of cloves and lines
etched into your palm, kissed
with no exhilarating lips, yes,
it will be a suffering,
this is the tao of the situation, bitterness,
balance achieved by the necessity
of lies, all these lingual guilts,
cruel, bitter, bite hard
this morning, by the window watching
the monsoon splatter itself against the panes,
I watched the neighbor children
splashing in the puddles, holding
plastic bags hoping to catch tadpoles
that will later turn to great
brown toads with lumps and peeling skins,
some days you get all the answers
and bitterness is a root, incriminating

and valuable, it approaches,
with glinting hooks swinging uncertainty,
linking the measure of evenness
and the weight of healing, all
hurling towards impotence, possessed,
barriers to superstitions, bitter, free
and for all to see.

Communion, Said The Barfly

There are so many good-looking men here tonight, did you meet anyone yet, I always meet bloody tourists who only wanna fuck, then love you long distance, make you stupid promises of going to Alaska together or Washington together, suck dick in Redwood HahaLand, did you meet anyone yet, what you like anyway, look at that one over there, I wanna fuck him, he looks sick though, sometimes I worry though, I want another drink, you want something, I met five guys in the last two days, all out-of-towners, no hope to find anyone who stays here in this provincial hick town, everybody is such pussyshit ugly trolls, I hate being troll bait, how can you stand it, I wanna leave this place, there's so many good-looking men around, don't call me by my real name, I don't want anyone to know, what do you drink.

Stick the dick bottle up your fuck nosehole and breathe like your nose up Mel Gibson's ass tasting his crack hairs and drinking it in till your tongue and spit taste like Ribena Pepto cough syrup minty mouthwash Listerine sting, don't spit into my mouth with that flavor breath and make your balls bust cock tip split and flow the cum in my face, anybody seen his poppers, no, he's a popper junkie can't cum can't rim can't fuck think about fucking without the smell of Liquid Paper thinner up his throat, climb into the dumpster to look for the last bottle while I lie in bed on my stomach press my dick hard into the mattress pretend it's him, wait till he comes back and puts rubbing alcohol to pep it up and he wants to fuck now, every part of his body wants to fuck now that it is ready to crack open his artery temples sinuses syndicated psychedelic orgasmic dreamworld nightmare wetcum dream life.

Oi woman get a life and get that peroxide poodle attacking your scalp off first stupid Chink woman thinks she's Haole wannabe fuck white eat white drink white shriek Oh look, look at all those short people, short people repeated like nobody gives a shit, gives me attitude bitch, try dying your crotch blonde and watch your pubic hairs fall out one by one.

I want to fuck the men who look like Jesus, fuzzy beards and chests, bless me Jesus with tattoos and pierced tits, pierced cocks, nipple clamps, nail the skin of my balls to your heavenly bed, make me cum in heaven baby, O angels sing primal piss in my mouth, clip my tits to Jesus's ring, rub my pubes into his, O show me no mercy merciful, O bless me, O fuck me godhead.

Pledging undying love with a gold ring inset with a diamond the size of an eyeball he says, Baby you can never have enough diamonds, Baby everlasting is a long time but is it real, Baby is it too big to be real, what's the point, Baby doesn't it end, is the rhythm wrong, Baby what can you do to make me love you.

Your cock is so ugly, it's so small and wrinkled, you can't fuck with it, it's only good for beating off, why are you so rude to me, is it some sort of racism, you don't know who you just fucked over, I'll have the cops on your tail, I'm not finished with you buddy, hey, fuck you buddy.

Die, Mr. Medallion Man, die. Take your Disco Divas with you, Mr. Medallion Man and die, die and leave us alone. Take your polyester and your Brut. Take your gold and your chains. Take your platform shoes and die, Mr. Medallion Man, die. You are Pisces, I am Virgo. You are Taurus, I am not. Take your astrology, take your flares and die. We will not be virgins no more for you. Our hymens, asses and sphincters have broken and you can't fix it, Mr. Medallion Man, so die. Take your haircuts and your thinly tapered shirts. Take your discos and your Bee Gees. Take your sideburns and your hairy chests. Take your Listerine Breath Spray, Mr. Medallion Man and die.

Will good-looking men love me when I die, will they press their hunky bodies against my dead ass, slowly lick my dead crack, shoot warm cum up on my cold lips, let the cum slip into the dead mouth, onto the tongue, O let my swollen tongue taste it, will they finger fuck my dead ass, will they huh, will they flex and pump their hard bodies so I can jerk-off dead cum, rub it into their shoulders, will they kiss me on the back of my neck and spit in the hollow of my throat, will they huh, will good-looking men love me at all when I'm dead?

He was a sailor but now he's a cab driver from Yugoslavia, why'd you have to blow him, why'd you have to suck him off while he took you home, lick his tits and play with his chest like you wanna fuck his dick, did you really enjoy it, George was a cabbie too, yeah in New York, got twenty bucks cos his passenger wanted to smell his shoes, got fifty bucks to smell his feet, why'd you have to suck him, why.

Sometimes your heart tastes better when you drown it in Buds and blow cigarette smoke through the cracks, patch the holes with cornnuts and popcorn pop trivia piss quiz birthday Carly Simon tunes, sometimes your heart feels much better when you cook it in KY Vaseline pot stogie puff blow paste and hang it up to dry beside Conair toasters yuppie heaven man, treat it good baby, love it like your CDs bonds and bedposts, treat it baby good, treat it next to your plague remover, kiss it baby, cos sometimes your heart sounds like rice cakes soaked in one part vodka, one part gin, one part Coke, one part Tutti Frutti Juicy, one part goo, one part jism, one part heaven, one part hell, one part fucking, one part fisting, one part AA, one part words, one part rimming, one part love.

Fate
(for Zack)

Fate comes straight
as my lover's neck,
stiff, off the bottle,
a line from my finger
tips to my eyes, by
way of the tendons
at the back of yr neck, taking
it smooth like opera
divas straining for that high
one. I got clots
the size of chestnuts
on my liver. Got the x-rays
to prove it. My balls are
swollen. Abnormal,
but you probably find it hot
even though I think I've lost
one of them far inside my body
cos nothing belonged to me: not
my shirt, not the loose change
jingling in my pocket, not the yawn
sniffle face, not even my feet,
but here I am. In the middle
of the downbeat where you
make it cos I am determined
to be the beloved in some
Marquezian romance with cocktail tooth
picks — no little tropical umbrellas.
You have to break the cycle of creeps.
All it takes is just one. Just
one and you're free for life.
The deal doesn't beat this
and I want it to be right.
        In the Book of Planets,
there are 12 ways to find
real love: The twelve-step
lovers-anonymous voodoo-magik
all to do with astrology

and stars, plotting
planets to decisively precise
arcs pointing to specific parts
of yr body. Copernicus couldn't
do better. Do it right
or one day you'll wake to find
that you've grown dry, scrambl-
ing for the last drops
of water, begging strangers
to spit into yr mouth or you
will become dust, unchallengingly
brown, swept away in an instant.
You won't like that, would you.
Pollen and grain will bind
you to nothing more
than you were without
so much as a desire to go on.
Your lover will be grammar,
shame, revenge, a bus
ride, a shampoo, late beyond help.
      Night will come and you
will settle under the animals
feet. Cobwebs will catch you.
Ants will eat you. You
will be nothing but teeth
& hair & bones, hollow
and sucking. Driven
into pages of tearoom
histories. Holding
hands only leads to sweaty
palms. Semen
betrays you to local
currency.

Risings

Sometimes, rising to eat
The moon is easy
When flowers sprout from
Marianne's eyebrows as she picks
Coins out of Edith Piaf's ears
Singing tears and mercy
Is no kind sister to us all,
Not anymore, never was, so
Come into the ghetto of my mind,
Sit on wooden planks and let's think
About how the moon rises and mates
With stars and how white angels
Eat each other with no table manners.
Don't point at the Big Dipper,
The Earth Mother will not like that.
Her bosom fuller than Liz's titillates
Fate and sometimes it is easy
Rising to eat the moon
When the moon is made of post-modern
Rhythmic lyric stanzas translated
From a foreign language, any language
Actually, tonight the moon
Is a stray cat with a macho attitude
Pissing where it pleases
And the spirit of Whitman
Has possessed Rupert the Bear.

Listen:
Planted on the hard tracks of this earth where the sweat of
    history holds my ankles, shackled, to the life bleeding
    into these grains and my lips cannot kiss the hardness
    and the brutishness of those hands that put us into the
    acid truth,
And truth is a smoky bay with turtle stools and jaded
    graying organisms sucking on sap, leach into the truth
    of the rush, the truth of altered blood is nothing more
    to me than a dip into the gravity of New Age karma,
The feel-good, the feel-goodness of the body sack pressing up
    my mouth, holding my tongue in a clamp, pickling what's

left of the reincarnation and I want to lie down once,
   sleep.

Stop that, Ms. Plath, you can't
Do that. Eat your green peas
And your french beans, eat your
Ovens and your gasoline, then spit
The seeds in your palm.
Call them different names
Of gemstones. Put them on your throat.
Think you're Jackie O,
eat a valium when you're done
Because sometimes
Sonny Rollins stands in
For the moon
And I want to climb on his horn
Slip into the metal and shiver
In the tone of worry
Because Cole Porter
Makes me sing happy
Ditties about uselessness,
Commercial diet Pepsi tunes
And I don't like it one bit
But he holds my head in violence
And splinters me
To pick his fingernails, his teeth
And Furry Lewis spits
My blood into spittoons
Not unlike those in grey Chinatown.

All together now:
   Dime eyes nickel breath
   Slip it in my crack
   Take my horny take my food
   Take my Mama's gunny sack
   Put it in the rice pot
   Put it in the fridge
   Let it fester let it stew
   Let it ripen while I rot.
Let's say this chant together.
Then make a yogurt dressing

And wrap it in lotus leaves,
Put a duck egg in the middle
And think of lives without
Anyone in them.
Call each name out loud
And let the new moon hear you.
Do this until the lunar month is up
Then wash your mouth with wine.
Now wait.
What you ask for will come true,
Our sweat is completed
The earth just wants us
This writing is our medicine
These ashes of our throats are our ceremony.

Flying the Red Eye

Flying the red eye with bodies breathing heavy all around me
    silent as cows strapped into corrals fed cleaned and fed
    again.
25G beside me has his tray table propped on his belly and is
    snoring but doesn't hear himself because his headset is
    loud on channel five.
He tells me that he travelled first class last year once
    because his sister's friend had connections and it was
    great champagne steak fresh fruit the works he says
    offering me his dinner roll *Jesus Christ this is hard as*
    stools ya want it.
The toilet is the only escape from the smoking section but
    there's pee everywhere it's hard to piss in turbulence and
    I miss too and I tell myself it's only six more hours.
Can't see any good clouds on the red eye and the stars are
    not out tonight or maybe they're there but I can't see
    them you see stars in first class I'm told but it's all
    darkness outside.
Airports are like bookends and planes they scare me big
    chunks of synchronized metal and plastic snatching people
    away from the earth.
The best kinds of airports are those where you don't have to
    walk where conveyor belts drag you to where you want to go
    because there's nothing worse than having to walk miles to
    throw someone on a plane then walk again to get them back.
I sit with the ferns with my carry-on luggage and wave
    goodbye to 25G beside me his sister is really quite sweet.
Cars pull up and people are flying into each other's arms and
    lips and little children bouncing in the backseat trying to
    grab daddy's baseball cap and dogs licking car windows and
    trunks opening and closing and french kissing and I am
    going home.

Positivity

Waking to find red spots
on my chest and arms
and rushing to the bathroom
to get into better light
to see if the spots
are raised bumps
or wet crusting sores

only to find,
they are flea bites

Getting sick is not fun
anymore. It used to be
lying in bed reading
good books while listening
to the radio and pampering
myself with fruits and juices
and really good confectionery

Now, every red spot
and every swollen gland
worries me. I start feeling
my glands all day
thinking they are becoming bigger
every time I touch them,

and looking for lesions,
skip the vaccination scar
and the post-operative scar,
maybe they're just insect bites

Getting sick these days
prompts well-meaning friends
to call and ask how I'm doing,
when *was* the last time,
and just *what* did I do.

Bestiality

Last night, the man with the grizzly white
beard told me to zip up
my fly: it was hanging open
and radio signals were coming
out. "Gotta be careful,
these days," he says
as he fills his eyelids
with cigarette butts and small bits
of paper he collects from the ground.
He spits up coffee beans, whole and shiny,
that's how he stays up, all night,
on the on-ramp, blocking traffic.
This one, he's pointing
people out to me, is loud.
"Cover yr ears or it will
become hemp, dead lice.
Hiya honey."

    "Lately I've been involved
with a spider. He's really neat.
He fits in the palm of my hand,
has eight legs which stretch
so good, sometimes

I forgets myself."

The End

The end is a kiss in the dark where I didn't want it
but I mmmed and ahhed anyway, in the yellow light
of another cheap hotel where
the greatest joke was the price of the humor, I

watch the cigarette burns in the hard orange carpet
fill with sweat and hair
the first day we fell and fucked and

fucked. Running naked down the hallway to the bathroom
on the other side, hoping no one would stick their heads
out of their door and see me running, me

with cum on my stomach, KY and blood
down my thigh. My crack opened
to show you nothing. Nothing

and you peed in it anyway and
my crack closed again. Later

sucking snuff in bed, reading Joe Orton by the small light,
looking out the frosted green glass, watching
the manager doing tai chi in the courtyard, watching
the city lights flicker off, and the sky fill

with the haze of another day, you
said I love you.

Pot

Where are the. Seatbelts. In the car. Where. Is your joint.
It. Is here. Do you want. Me to. Light it.
At 90. Miles. Per hour. Weaving. Around. The windows.
With the sweet. Smoke.
The stash. Is not. Where it should. Be. In the drawer. It. Is on the floor.
The rabbits. Can get to. It.
Have you. Cured. Your infection. Did you. Wash. I don't.
Want. To suck you.

Night

The light from the street lamp shines
through the window and shades your face.
In this dull shadow, you look different,
disfigured like the gargoyles I saw
at the museum today; it was
a visiting exhibition, next week
there will be something from South America.

As you sleep, cradled in my body,
your breathing is rhythmic. Listening
to your soft breath, I breathe
in time with you, counting the number
of breaths each minute, 17.

You look so small when
you're asleep. I wonder
what you're dreaming, and if you'd remember
the dream when you wake.

I dreamed of Dorothy Parker.
She came to me and said *bitch*; then
spiders gathered around me. Dorothy
Parker was wearing a dress with spider prints
on it. I thought it was curtain material.
I woke and saw your monster features
tucked in me and I was frightened. I
wanted to scream but did not want to wake you.

The clock glares its red eyes at me
and says *sleep*.
I glare back and say *count the time, count*.
The clock says *I will*.

A woman looks in from the window,
she doesn't say a word; I think
she is crying. She stands and we look
at each other for a while before she melts
into the shape of a spider on the window,
lost, homeless, and probably hungry.

I offer it my blood to suck but it declines;
it only wants blood from flying organisms.
I cannot fly
even if in dreams I flew
off a tall blue building, listening
to Patsy Cline records. I glided
for a while, then plummeted to my sheets,
wet and shivering.

The cat enters the room, looks
at us. He jumps on the bed, licks his paws
and smiles at me like he knows something
I don't. He winks at me, blows me a kiss, moves
to the window, kills the spider with a swat
of his paw, yawns and disappears through the window.
I see him flying upward, soaring like
a plastic toy aeroplane.
He tells me of the neighborhood
in the darkness of the nearly morning,
the little contained in each shoebox, all
kitty litter, all waiting
for the morning, to
be taken all away.

Bangkok

He wants to impress you that he is different.
Not like those catalogued parading
thin brown boys with poofy haircuts
and numbers sticking to their butts,
trying to look happy, sexy
for fat old fairies with fat wallets

of American dollars. No, he is different,
he says, in a postcard with a picture
of a river in front, he is looking sexier
each day. Please hurry, buy me a pair of Levi's
then we can go traveling together.
He is not one of those boys

you meet in the bar who will go with you
for two nights straight, then tell you
that his brothers are starving because
his mother, sisters and aunt are ill
with some infectious disease. *Please just
twenty American dollar is okay to*

help. He is not one of those ten-dollars-a-pop boys
either. No, he is not for rent. He only wants
to make you happy. Make you smile, like
everyone else here does. One big smile-fest. Smile
at every damn thing because everybody gets
what they want, if they know how, here.

Crabs From A Gun

They are Harry Winstons in a bed of hair.
A spray of water trapped frozen,
                    then they move
like little spiders move with purpose
with nowhere to go.
            I am amazed
how they travel from you to me
with their slow fluid motions
when your strands rubbed against into mine:
so invisible you could put your hand through
me and I through you and still come up
with nothing, after all this time
I travel with your blood,
sweat, tears, semen, saliva
tattooed, tapewormed inside me.
They are moving again,
            they eat
into my flesh. If I were them,
they would be cannibals.

I pull one from the warm safety of its nest,
lay it on the table, press
him with the tip of a drawing pen,
hear him pop and stop moving.
                It is odd
being transparent, to let
the whole seeing world eye your insides
and to die with a pop
like it was nothing special.

I will remember it is easy
this span of life
that we wrap ourselves in
        chaotically neat,
it is the art of falling apart
that I know of.
I will collect the pieces of my body,
lay them down and let
them be.

The Ballad of Dependency
(for Lisa)

My nose is like a dog. Every morning, I sniff out the correct key from the cluster in my pocket, sniff out the keyhole and open the heavy swinging smudged glass doors to let the fumes of the teak racks and the leaking corks attract them.

They come like flies, bleary eyes ripped open through the sleep-eyed paste that seals, stick, stuck to their eyelashes, all drooling, smacking their lips as they stand around, caressing the shiny glass, opening the refrigerator door and watching the vapor condense on the cool bottles, wetting the labels they don't read, can't read anyway. It's all intuition that they pick up the right bottle and bring it to me smiling their platinum Visa smiles, gold Amex smiles. I give them salvation with their signatures and they are thankful. They cradle the brown bag as if it were a newborn baby still wet and dripping through the paper sack and slink off to sip their drip bags in serene satisfaction.

Today, one of them drops a bottle from his shaky hands. He stands and looks at the puddle of liquid and cracked glass spreading on the floor, looking guilty like he just peed in his pants in public. The face all blank as he stares at his hemorrhage. The fumes of the liquid make me want to vomit. I tell him to leave. He is not welcomed here anymore. The excommunication from his church of poison is too much for him. I mop the mess up with a rag, strain the cloth through a coffee filter three times, extract the baptismal waters, put it in a clean glass and drink it. I sweep the floor. I swear the dust smells like Chivas and lunch today, $3.95 spaghetti and meat sauce, tastes like Johnny Walker. It slips down so easy and grows snaky in my gut, all sliding over each other, trying to find my asshole, my mouth or nose to slither out their relief. Standing on my feet settles me: If anything happens, I'm already on my feet and can run like hell. Do you believe in bottled genies? They can look like Barbara Eden in harem pants, pink ass bobbing, giggling, "Oh Master, I promise to be good, Master," or the Persian kind with turbans and sabers granting three wishes, no more, can't use a wish to wish for more wishes. Sometimes I hear the genies clinking away against the sides of the bottles in no time, tune or tempo. Not all bottles have genies, you got to have the luck to know which one, you got to be a pro. Sometimes I let a genie out, just for fun, no wish, nothing. What can I want, ever. It's all here, liquefied for easy swallowing. It's in the air. I can just breathe it, dust my nose with it. Even a baby can feed itself here. It's so easy. Released genies slip away quietly between the cracks in the floor boards or are absorbed in the walls. Genies who grant a wish disintegrate on the spot. I wish for time. Just like in that song endless played on easy listening. Nothing happens and another genie disappears. Can't wish for something you already got but nobody bothers to tell you the goddamn rules, dammit. You just got to know for yourself, day after day. Raid the garbage cans, pee at the crosswalks, shit on the pavements. Nothing to tie you down. No rules, it's so easy to be fine, to figure it all out.

A History of Geography

America is a place far away,
as far as London/ Australia/ or Canada
any Western country where people speak English,
All a page in an atlas/ a place on a map, can't drive/ walk/
    take a bus to —
I want to go there, so I buy magazines, take a Biro felt pen,
    draw arrows to people in the photographs & write my name
    on their foreheads,
I want to go there so I fuck their people,
don't care if they're good-looking/ or turn me on or not,
I let them take me,
do what they want with me
even if it hurts me bad/ makes me bleed/ makes me bruise/ sore/ & angry/
sad/ satisfied/ & happy/ mad/ desolate,
let them do what they want with a slab of meat
because they're giving me a place I cannot get to.
So I throw my legs up in the air,
spread them in toilets/ spread them in parks/ spread them in
    hotel rooms,
rich hotels/ with real fancy sheets and bedspreads/ with mint
    chocolates and strawberries by starched white pillows &
    fancy room service/ & nice uniformed bellmen/ &
    receptionists who look at me and know what I'm doing/ cos
    they want to do it too/ done it before,
maybe cheap rundown hotels/ with shared bathrooms & thin
    walls/ creaky beds/ bed lice & stinking men.
But I don't care cos I'm in America/ in London/ in Australia/
    in France/ in anywhere but this town.
This town where I am the son of a generation/ lost
to 25 years of what price paradise.
This town so clean and green, everything wiped over with
    Dettol every week,
wiped so clean, they take away your insides
& give you dog biscuits & standard rations to replace what
they've disinfected.

I hold things I cannot say in my mouth,
I hold acts I cannot do in my chest,

hold a bitter stinking love in my groin.
Let them wipe away everything else,
wipe me/ disinfect me/ hose me down,
but I got what nobody else got
and they can't wipe that away
not even with their industrial strength bleach.
& I don't/won't care what they make me sing/chant *justice,*
     equality, peace, progress, prosperity, happiness for my
     life,
it's all words that I sing/ chant/ move my lips/
know what it means,
and that is dangerous.
Wrap myself in newsprint,
wrap myself in satellite transmissions,
wrap myself in truth/ lies/ truth/ half truths,
believe what I wrap myself in knowing
I cannot go back.

They want to distill me,
take the queer sky out of my body.
Let it sit, simmer until my fire burns up in itself.
& when I am dark/ when I have no more light/ when I am no
     more an abomination/ when I am no more shame/ when I am face
     again/ when the collective being of me worships god, family,
     education and the collective administrative silver spoon,
then I will be back in the fold.
The prodigal child, back from exile.

Please let me live
and rage in the realm of wonderment,
to know that the hand in the glove is not the fascist halal
     rationed kiss that makes me feel like a stranger/ an
     outsider in my own.
Let me live in all that my blood is mine,
in the color of spirits
backwards.

I am blind,
     born blind, spirits come to me in polaroids of abstract
     paintings that throw mud and saliva on my eyes to see
     the new issue of Blue Boy,

who show me that love is deaf,
        born deaf, spirits come to me as a bluesy lullaby, a
        cat's howl at night that fills my ears/ that I can't
        hear/ don't want to hear/ whispers yes that chokes me
till I can't speak, born dumb,
spirit is a voice that no one will hear because everybody is
        born deaf, dumb and blind
in the bright lights holding us in a circle jerk, to the
        music we speak of nothing that cannot find our minds.
& I am in this world of pirates, prayers, ascensions, coups,
        attacks, counterattacks, shadows, illness, deceptions,
        manipulations, addictions, metaphysicians, hyperboles,
        poetics, politics, plays, perspiration and love.

Flesh/Wound

The air slices my teeth. Another year has past, and I am swimming
so fast that now I am swimming very fast.
—Lisa Asagi, *The Midnight Sun*

Once upon a time I would have loved you so deep and so savage that
you would have given up your family name like a desperate man nervously
hawking his mother's wedding ring at a cheap pawn shop: all at once sweating
and swearing that it was real it was his & it was good. Once upon a time
underneath a lifetime of the sweetest dreams as dense as night waves as strong
as undercurrents you would have known what it was to be loved like that.
But now, only fate can kiss you like I would: wet, stinging and so tender you
would beg for just one more.

Everybody looks at me and all they see is nine hard thick inches attached
to low hangers that whisper *Jeff* into their ears as I fuck them in the ass
without a word without lube without a rubber and without waiting for them
to cum after I finish, all the while staring straight at point X where the camera
should be.

All but you, Edward, you know what this is all about. I know you do. I
know you as one of the buttfuckers buttfucking your way to some semblance
of respectability; like me. I know that when you touch me, when I feel your
soft hands — unblemished by rough blue collar concerns, except for that
callous where the riding crop cut into your palm and your doctor said it was
just a flesh wound — when you run your hands on my body, I know you're
saying my name over and over *Mary Jo, Mary Jo...*, my name and nothing
else because what can you say to me that I haven't heard anyway? That I
don't already know is a pure 80-proof lie? What can you say that you aren't
too terrified to say? What words wouldn't hold you by the balls and twist?
I'm just another flesh wound in your life, Edward. Do I deserve more?

Sometimes I lie in bed beside you and your newlywed and watch you
toss in a fretful sleep, watching your hands — no, not your hands, your
fingers, only your fingers twitch, as if you were clawing for air, for the
beginning of a breast stroke, for meniscus — and your blushing bride lying
beside you, oblivious to your erosion, dreams her proper New England
dreams that were to have been mine in the first place. There is hell somewhere
in this world. And I think that we have been the closest to it than anyone in
America. You gave it to me and I gave it back to you again and again like a
party game; when the music stops, who will be left holding it all?

Not me, not Mary Jo. Are you begging for one more caustic smooch?

There was this movie. A man meets this woman, he's utterly smitten by her. He obsesses about her. He follows her around. One day, while spying on her as she undresses, he sees someone hiding in her apartment. He thinks it's some kind of game. A sex game created by two lovers and immediately he gets hard. But then, it's too late when he realizes that the man is actually a murderer and kills his obsession as he watches horrified through his binoculars all the while with one hand nesting in his fly.

You can find this movie at Tower Video in the Midnight Movie section which is usually located beside the porn. I know because one day, I wanted to show a friend an early tape of mine that I didn't have a copy of. The store didn't have the tape and I ended up with this movie instead. After that, for weeks, I'm thinking what it would be like if some racist fag-bashing psycho killer gets off on killing me while his nazi skinhead lover watches from across the street and masturbates, saving his jism for no one but the floor.

Edward likes musicals. They're a safe thing to like. No chance of reporters or the cheesy tabloids getting hold of some sick politically incorrect movie that he was hot for, he says. Edward likes *South Pacific* best. *Happy talking happy talk...* I once heard Edward singing in the shower one afternoon. He likes to leave the door slightly ajar, something he really couldn't do at home because it wasn't proper. He's singing and I'm lying in bed, the spread and blanket kicked to the floor, the undersheet strategically placed to absorb and cover the wet spots that the hotel maids will deal with the next morning, but to them, these will be like any of the thousands of cum-stained sheets in any one of the 18,000 hotels in the state that must be laundered, not Kennedy cum wasted on some cheap trick. When Julio Iglesias slept in Princess Grace's castle, the castle staff fought to be the ones to wash Julio's underpants. (Apparently, all laundry at the castle were handwashed.) But in the good ol' U.S. of A., or anywhere else for that matter, Kennedy cum holds no weight in a hush-hush fuck than it would if Joe Sixpack sneaks a blowjob in a park: If a tree falls in the woods and Edward fucks me on its dead trunk, did I feel it? Did he cum?

Once flying, we met Linda and Jerry en route to Cancun. Two more hours till touchdown and two bottles of tequila down, Linda looks at me straight with tears in her brown eyes and says, "Baby, you gotta know when to pull out when you've had enough." Jerry closes his eyes, says, "Amen." But then, once upon a time who knew what a blind fluid desire could do to a person? Who knew how much was enough? Not me, not Jeff. I would have gripped you in a leglock and held you fast, letting you cum right deep inside of me even though it would feel like cancer, smell like a burning.

You know how it is to create life from scratch, spin dazzle damage control. To crawl out of the primeval slime, out of the swamp, and walk to freedom, walk home. Porn and politics aren't all that different when you finally draw the lines. All it comes down to is the clothes and the bodies. But the flesh, the attitude, the sincerity and the ability to look into the camera and stick your dick into the right hole blindly, but still hitting the spot every time as folks at home gripping their hard-ons, their remote controls, afraid to hit the forward button or the channel changer, believe that you're the only one who can save them from drowning. Everyday I'm drowning and you hold me down under your spit and I can't breathe but I trust you so much that I know you will save me just before my lungs burst and everything but air fills my body. Don't forget to pull out for that cum shot: that's what makes the money, the fantasy.

In spite of all that's happened, I still love bridges. I love being suspended over a greatest expanse of water only trusting two points that hold it all up. Once, I wanted to film a scene on a bridge: Me as the maintenance worker who fucked a poor hapless motorist stranded on the bridge played by this young underage kid who had the proper I.D. to keep himself working. Only thing was that the company couldn't get permission to shoot a film, any film on the bridge, but it all would have been so hot.

I've discovered bungee jumping, the real kind — off a bridge, not some silly crane that dangles you above the municipal parking lot. The real kind lets you dip your head into water before whipping you back up into the air and you hang upside down until someone comes to rescue you, cut your straps, pull you to safety, all in midair; air less dense than water: it's a simple scientific fact that you can figure out with common sense even if you don't know the terminology.

In spite of conventional wisdom, you *can* drown in air: and compared to water, it's more painful and not one scrap of your flesh will be spared.

Edward. Cut me loose. Set me free.

Once upon a time I would have danced in dark prisons to free you. Would have defended you, swinging the heavy rubber replica of my dick, big and ready to kill anyone who would dare wrong you.

But now I'm running as fast as I can, as fast as the lactic acid and oxygen in my leg muscles will allow me, as fast as I can breathe. I'm afraid to look back, but like Lot's wife, I do, and instead of salt, I turn. into. calm. blood.

Do you know what it's like to take it up the ass?

The Secret Life of Flowers

I.

The secret life of flowers pressed between the pages of *Gulliver's Travels* and the *Encyclopedia Britannica*. I open the pages to read petals. They are pianos. Play them hard and mad. Step on them. They will unfold, splendid parsnips. Pollen smothers babies. Shape your mouth like a humming bird's beak. Draw out nectar with your new mouth. I am relieved, of course. A narrative. A four-course aspirin meal. Stick insects the size of aeroplanes. Wind them up like rubber bands. Release them and watch them spin. Flowers walk like penguins. Shakily the stone creaks.

II.

Sunflowers have eyes. Like flies. Millions of compound eyes. Ripple when you spread your hand across them. It is bubble pack. Brush their eyelashes with a comb. Decide the color of eyeshadow. Is mascara wise? The sunflowers are watching the children play. See the sunflowers strangle the children. See the children choke and die. Blue bits on the grass oh no. See the sunflowers eat the children. Look at the sun and say ah. Is the sun a star? It is a gaseous ball. What is a planet? The sunflowers bow to the sun. Kiss their roots. Lips filled with mud and stones. Sing Hallelujah.

III.

Flowers are violent. Sleep, they will slap you. Fill your nose with nectar and rosewater. Dream of drowning in beeswax. Sting your body with the arms of thorns. White roses kiss death. Yellow roses kiss rape. Pink roses kiss suicide. Red roses kiss themselves. When you hear the sound of roses, know that the ceiling was too low.

IV.

Flowers are the book of S. Form it with your mouth. In the dictionary, find the book of S. Say subterranean over and over. Singing acid in the rain. The tune of violins. The lines of niceness. Say *swing, swivel*. You are chrysanthemums. Brew yourself. Break each petal. Release the ant in each of them. Ants live around my bed. They crawl up the walls. I kill them. Little ant bodies on my sheets. Last night, they climbed onto my chest & made a nest. Sixty seven thousand ant-lives in my chest. I shall shower. Kill them.

V.

I am the day of openness. Hold the globe between your hands. Spit out the stupidity of carnations. The carnations will rule. Scepter & crown are translucence. Let in light & relax. Distant guns feel like the hum of the earth. Weave for two or three minutes. Reciprocate the curious pearls. Bright red carnations labeled WORSHIP. Carnations will military you. You must wave when carnations pass by. Smile. They can see you. They want your money. Carnations will pierce their ears. Buy them long dangling earrings. With rhinestones. Bougainvilleas are foreign. What language do they speak? Hibiscus are subversive. Rebels. Sulphurous acid and coriander say free. Carnations control Chrysler. I want to drive a Buick. Knowing what parallels is a technique. It grows from seeds the size of egos. Plant them. Water them. Watch them. Children.

VI.

The anthropology of flowers is skulls. Bones. The bridge to kingdom come. Flowers are Satan's tool. Evil. There are no flowers in Hell. They are on Earth. I shall eat flowers till I explode. Eat irises as asparagus. Boil lilies with pepper and MSG. I open my hand. Irises are pillows. Herb baskets of living things. Irises in the oven are angry. I fill myself with the anger of flowers. I say grace and dine on zinnias. Angry daisies. The revolution flowers is inevitable. Flowers are murder. Cold-blooded bludgeoning. You will not feel a thing. Evaporation is the key to overthrow. I am counting veins. Hibernate. You will know how flowers sleep. Do flowers dream? Wash flowers in alcohol. Put two drops behind your ears. Think it is Chanel No. 5. They will not disturb you, they say. Lilies are jealous. Radioactive.

VII.

I hate you baby for being plumeria. Why did you do that to me? Were they birth pains for you? Rise out of your sea. Lie at my feet. Shortness is ugly. A Detroit mustache in Hawaii. The flowers know that. They speak to grapes a lot. Days are stamens. Feathery. Bait with ambition. Crystals laugh as they plot your end. Mine is reassured. Oh rain & dew drops. Oh greenness. Stop it. Flowers accompany me. They are friends. Spiteful. Flowers attach themselves to me like warts. Hello, earth. Are my eyes open or closed? I know it is sunflowers. They have eyes, don't they? Don't put that periwinkle on me. Is it agony? Is it a cure for cancer? Shall I drink it? Balance flowers with sweet and sour cream. Break the silence. It is driving me insane. Is it moist? Fall into the mirror. Will Jane be coming? Dive into the vast. Indeed repeated endlessly. Can you say talking succession? I am a black sleeve. Chips on the floor. Respectability. I am the secret life. Do you know me?

Sold

Sold

One toot means lunch, two toots means quitting time.
You'll get the hang of it.
Just take this knob thing here, screw it to this flap-
thing here,
and put the whole thing in this tray, here.
You'll get the hang of it.
Do it today, tomorrow, week after, next year, and
you can do it blindfolded with one arm one leg while
chewing gum and whistling Dixie.
All at the same time.
Here have some. Do you chew gum?
Passes the time you know.
Me I chew gum and imagine the boyfriend's hand up my thigh.
You got a boyfriend? Should see mine.
You'll want his hand up your thigh too.
Gee, I love your hair. What do you do with it?
Mine's hopeless. A head of pubic hair.
What conditioner do you use?
Gum sorta stops you from going on the munchies.
See Row-6-#-3-Mathilda there?
Two years ago she looked like Zsa Zsa Gabor young.
Acted like she was too.
Now pig-woman. Gum passes the time you know.
Here have some. Do you chew gum? You got a boyfriend?
I love your hair? What conditioner do you use?
Do you like movies? A bunch of us go to the movies Thursday.
Or maybe go bowling. But mostly we go movies with happy endings.
We like love stories. We like to have a good cry.
Do you like movies? Do you like gum?
Do you want your boyfriend's hand up your thigh?
Do you have a boyfriend?
You'll get the hang of it.
Put the whole thing in this cart here. Passes the time.
What do you do with it? One toot lunch.
Zsa Zsa Gabor at Row-6-#-3. Pig-woman with 6 kids. Do you chew gum?
Today, tomorrow, week after you'll get the hang of it.
One long toot means fire drill. If you're lucky.
We get to go to the courtyard and gossip.
Two toots quit one long toot gossip one toot lunch.

You'll get the hang of it. I love your hair.
Do you like movies? Maybe bowling with a good cry?
What gum you use? Here have some.
Put the whole pig-woman in this cart, here.
I love your movies with a good cry and happy endings.
Munchies stops you going tomorrow. Lunch toot.
Boyfriend toot. Movie toot. Bowling toot. Happy endings toot.
Pig-woman toot. Gum chewing toot. Fire toot.
Flap-thing-knob-thing toot.
You'll get the hang of it.

State

The walls
are whiter than they were
yesterday.
Watch them move
around.

I am 15:
braces and polyester
shorts two inches
above the knee;
I roll the band
so it will be short
like the guys
at school.

4 years;
it is no different, sitting
in this piss-stained
     shit-stained
stall, trying
to convolute
the meanings
     philosophies of life
while watching
the foot behind that wall,
watch it move and
speak to it
     with you,
and you will leave me:
It is a feeling,
     I name it
so I can speak of it,
I feel
taste it.
I live it:
a child
to be 30
and have validity

        to wake
in the alcohol
state, afternoon,
don't know where
I/you are.

Pump
a cockroach full
of drugs booze
and watch it climb
the walls.

This Is Your Life

Not much, is it?
After dumping cement
on the bits of lawn she can't reach
with her old lawnmower, she goes
to her sons' room, sits on the edge
of their bed with tears in her eyes,
points to Jesus on the wall.
        *Pray. When you're scared
        of the dark, just look at him.*
She kisses them goodnight
and makes sure they have their socks on.
Five months later, the picture of Jesus is gone.
She discovers that it violated
"thou shall not worship any graven image"
it's sinful and the picture disappears one day.

This is her life.
She paints the doors and cupboards black
so the dirt won't show.
But dust is white and that
still shows.

Now, she sips iced tea and wonders
why her sons are so distant.
One who is so scared of himself that he crumbles
like an almond cookie.
The other who loves his fag-self so much, it hurts
her. *Pray, walk close to the lord.*

She remembers them growing up
differently. Now, she realizes
why one could never speak to her,
why he always turned silent when she spoke
of *God's punishment to sinners.*
She tells them of all the sacrifices
she made for them, how
they must make her proud and how much they do
make her proud. Is it not so much to ask for?
It is late now, this is her

life and the stuffed bears collecting dust
and sunlight, the empty beds,
the same vague letters and the old
photographs can't hold her in place.
Clinging to her bible and daily devotions, prayers
and church work, this is her life.
Ask her how she's living it.

Tied

This is a tin-mining town with just one traffic
light at the town square and floods
every December, guaranteed,
and you're just another one
of the women in this town
who raises her kids, takes care
of the house and helps her husband at the shop.
You don't know better
when your husband brings home
the town seamstress as his second wife,
She gives birth to two kids.
You raise them as your own
and they know it too.
They call you Ma & Ah-Ma,
and they call her Mother.
What reason has she got to be jealous of you?
What does she know about childbirth?
You've done it thirteen times,
watched four of them die.
Your friends have all left
since the bottom fell out
of tin, years ago. They've moved
to the big town now. Your children
have all grown and moved too.
Now, you're tied down to your husband
since his stroke. What do you know
about business? About running
a pig farm? You let the second wife
take over the business.
She tells the old man you slander
her, poison her children's minds
against her. What can you do?
The old man takes her side.
What does she know about
taking care of the old man?
All day, you're cooking his favorite
dishes for him, feeding him, washing him, amusing him.
Your children tell you to leave.
Sell the house and bring the old man

to town where he can stay with them.
But he won't let you. He wants to live here,
in this tin-mining town where
everything shuts down, closes up
at 5:30 p.m. What do you know
about leaving? Where have you ever gone?
You hide the money your children give you.
You know the second wife takes the money
the children give to the old man.
She'll take yours too, if she could.
She tells him she will send it back
to the village for him.
You know the old man doesn't trust anyone with his money.
He knows his second wife steals his money.
He starts keeping his money in his shirt pocket.
The first time you have money of your own.
What do you do with your money?
You spend it during Chinese New Year,
and for your grandchildren's birthdays.
You buy a new color TV for the house.
You lie and say your children bought it
for you. Now, the old man watches the news
and anything that's on TV. Now, you have time
to make quick trips to the neighbors'.
You know that is not enough.
You want to play cards with your friends,
spend your evenings watching those never-ending Cantonese serials,
visit your children in different towns,
live in different states,
wash the pork smell and the smell
of the old man's vomit off your hands,
but you can't, you're still tied down, here,
in this tin-mining town with one traffic light
and annual floods. In December,
you have your chickens, raised from eggs,
and your cat to worry about.

Bar Poem

The man wants to know what the song is.
It's the last song on the first side of the tape.
I don't know. I don't like it. It's called *Whole Lotta Trouble*.
He takes a pen out of his pocket.
He writes the name of the song on a slip of paper.
We're talking about Chinese herbs now.
The barmaid says *they're so sweet smelling*.
She could smell them all day.
The blonde beside me smiles.
She remembers what Chinese herbs smell like.
I think Chinese herbs smell awful.
I remember whole shops of bottles, herbs, horns, nauseating.
The phone rings. The barmaid says *Hello, yeah?*
The man is back. He's talking about CDs, records and tapes.
He likes records best of all. He likes their roundness.
He wants to know about the album on the box.
Man, this is a song I can relate to.
I say it's so-so.
The barmaid is back. She likes the album. She plays it all day.
The blonde sees someone she knows.
She goes to talk to the woman who has just come in.
The woman has a scarf around her shoulders.
It is a scarf with an Indian print.
The man says the print is *interesting*.
He blows the smoke from his cigarette to the ceiling.
The ceiling is kinda dirty. It has stars painted on it.
The barmaid asks the man for a cigarette.
He gives her one. She lights it. She pretends she's a sex goddess.
The blonde is back. The woman wasn't very friendly.
The woman wants to be left alone. She's got a beautiful scarf.
The song on the box finishes. The barmaid plays the album again.
I want another drink. I don't care for the album.
I don't like cigarette smoke.
The barmaid turns the TV on.
There's a football game on. No one's interested. She turns it off.
The blonde says the woman smells like Chinese herbs.
Chinese herbs smell like cigarette smoke I say.
The blonde looks at the woman.
She is alone. She is drinking a whiskey.

The blonde lights a cigarette. The man offers me one.
I don't smoke. I don't like cigarette smoke. I want to leave.
The barmaid is complaining about her feet.
I tell her to use insoles. I'll bring some for her next time.
We kiss goodbye.
The blonde wants to kiss me goodbye. I kiss her.
The man wants to kiss me goodbye. I kiss him.
He laughs and shakes my hand.
The night is quite cold. My coat is wet.
My neighbor's dog is fucking someone's dog.
My cat's asleep on the bed.
My mother called and said to call her. I will.
I turn on the radio. They're playing a song.
It is the song on the box. I sing along with the song.

Luck

The hen must be fresh, as young as possible,
when it is cooked. This is how it's done:
hack off its legs so that it can't run away,
then lay a piece of cement on the fluttering body
to keep it still until it is ready to be bled.
Slit the neck with a sharp knife.
Collect the blood: a delicacy.
Rip off the feathers, gut the bird and wash
thoroughly so that the skin gleams
when you bring it to the pot of simmering herbs and spices.

Like everything else, there is a right way
to kill a chicken for the dinner table.
It is not for the squeamish or for those who
question the cycle of power, wondering
who decides, who takes up
where others leave off
and what holds it all together as neatly
as Lana Turner's hair, not one strand,
one wisp out of place.

This is what perfection is.
Being able to dissect yourself
so clearly the edges threaten like paper cuts.
Square everything away.
Give the gizzards to the cats, the bones
to the soup stock. The white meat. The dark meat.
It all falls into place
as night and day, clean and easy.
Ready to be packed up and taken by the mail carrier
at any moment's notice. Quietly. Without hassles.
No pain. Better than morphine.
There is nothing left to do, but to
take the eggs. Hard-boil them.
Dye them red. They're for luck.

The Bridegroom

This is our wedding night,
we have to do what we're supposed to do.
I didn't have anything to do with it all
I didn't know it was you or who you were
my fingers were cramped
and I pointed to the picture closest
I could reach
and the families sighed:
no more face lost,
I will not be trouble anymore.

Maybe I stood too long at the piss tanks,
maybe I looked too long at the man beside me,
maybe I looked into his eyes and saw
what I thought he saw in mine;
I saw the want of another man,
the love and satisfaction and teachings
only one man can give to another;
he saw hate.

They came from nowhere,
interrogated me as if they didn't know why
I was there and why they were there;
see my lips?
They were once so beautiful
so full and perfectly shaped
you could eat them,
can't you tell anymore?
They forced me to smoke unfiltered cigarettes
until the glowing tip inched like a millipede
into my face, into my mouth, into my lips,
they beat me, took away my clothes
and put me in a cell with twenty other men,
murderers, thieves, criminals.

I tried to hide my shivering body
by undressing the other men,
I see them taking off their clothes
giving me their warm jerseys, putting it on me,
their black nipples and tight curled pubic hairs

were more beauty than I could bear confronting me,
their tattoos were my friends,
their tattoos were hate,
and their eyes were hate;
they knew why I was there
they were told why I was there
and they wanted to hurt me
have their way with me;
ass pussy, it's the same for them
who will be killed this week, next month,
next year, anytime anyway;
but were afraid I was diseased.

Don't be angry with me
I don't know what all this means
I am tired and I want to get this life over with
so come to me, my beautiful picture bride,
come, let us consummate this marriage.

Swoop

These days I wake in the scabbed light
of damaged goods and benevolent memories.
There is my fear of speaking,
my fear of questions.
My young frightful past.

Should I find myself in your familiar arms
again?
    Your vast scrape of skin, warmer
than the blankets, and the cat
curled at our feet.
        You explained how you need
to leave one leg sticking out
of the covers to keep your body
temperature comfortable

    & I realized how
might my body get accustomed to sleeping
one more night knowing your heavy limb
may never crash across my bed.

In the same flash of late-night television,
insomnia and skewed biorhythms in which I discovered
the utter pleasure of falling upward
into the clash of your breath and the warmth
contained in your sleeping body, I wake
to errant light, realizing
that you're 350 miles to Los Angeles,
on your way to another lover.
I cannot revise all that has transpired
even though I want to swoop in
at the 100-mile point to tell you,
"My tongue memorizes the path to the soft
spot, the hollow in your neck that nudges
me back when you taste the tips of my fingers,"

    at the 200 milestone, I dive in to croon
"I have cultivated the shadows of my body,
of my life into tough spots where you may sleep

and not be easily crushed,"
        at 300 miles, I say
"The curve of your hip
is well mapped by my thorns.
My tender belly adores you,"

at 349, you will know
I never once belied my multitude
of passions, nor thought yours
foolish nor vain.

If you keep driving,
that one last mile,
            understand that
I have never felt anything this close before.

& if you don't stop,
I will know how to.

Bergamot

In the beauty shop, the saleswoman dabs
a touch of bergamot to my right wrist;
I grind the spot staining
my thin skin and vulgar veins
stretched across my carpus to the left
of its image; the friction
spreads the scent into my pulse
and I bring my newly aromatic
joint to my face.

    This was before I knew the name
of that heady scent spilling
from teacups filling cafés
in steam and clink of pastry plates.
Before how the smell of a big pot
of chicken soup cooking in my kitchen
changed. Before I knew how
perfumous desire was, before I knew
the whiff of missing a lover.

Hypothermia
(for Adam)

Stranded mountaineers have been known to lie
in the slit bellies of their pack animals,
crouched in the vapor of warm blood
to prevent hypothermia; the human body being
that frightfully fragile pack
of skin, flesh, organs, bones,
one fierce dip in temperature
and it betrays without even a kiss;

when rescuing cattle trapped
under ice, farmers have been known
to draw warmth from the animals' ears;
that last night I woke with your warm slab
of body next to me, your strong arm
draped heavy over my chest, the piercing,
a metal bar across the lobe of your right ear,
pressing into the back of my neck,

one small touch of the cold night
measured against ambivalence, mixed
emotions. Leaning into your still sleeping
body, I gently fondled your stiff ears, nuzzled
my lips against the stubble of your head,
followed the flicker of your tattoos
as it crossed mine like a game of Snakes
& Ladders; one false move and you fall

down the slippery scaled back of a snake,
back to the start, back to Square One,
to finding your way around the game
of boys pretending to be men and men
never knowing what it ever was like
to be boys, finding where you fit in,
where I fell out; and hearing your voice
on the phone again after all that time,

remembering that one last fling, I know
that a clear and present memory is another

trick of staying warm, another way
to keep holding for that one lucky throw
that will allow me to scramble up a long
sturdy ladder where perhaps we'll find something
definite, real time, hard proof,
unapologetically waiting there.

Zoo Animals

The Snow Leopard, the regal,
once illusive monster becomes
a freak show, family entertainment;
who'd have thought eating
flesh could excite so much.
But here, at feeding time,
caged out of his wild home,
taunted with crunchy children all day,
little scampering treats just out of reach,
his fat precise paws unable
to swipe through metal bars, unable
to attend to the scent

of fresh kill, we smell
his hunger and his sadness.

The sweating penguins airing their armpits
in their Cleopatra reed-lined pool.
The red-assed monkey clinging to its wire cage
pulling his butt hairs out.
The polar bear with skin allergies
gnawing on his arm.
The zoo holds its share of denizens
negotiating their language of pride.
You tried to hold my hand
at the gorilla compound;
I pulled away.
Even though I wanted
to put my arms monkey-like around you,
I haven't mastered the art
of publicly displaying affection.
I'd rather not have anyone see me;
one of our differences, the ability
to be looked at without flinching.

At the Insect Zoo
you squat on the floor
to ask the kid if he had ever seen
a Malayan beetle. *Yeah, they're everywhere*

in summer, he says; he lives in Petaluma,
little chance of sighting such an exotic insect.
I don't confuse the Californian and the Malayan
of the species, have stomped
on the latter in my slippers as a kid, delighting
in how they pop and splatter their bug juice.
But here, the targets of my childish cruelty,
lay under glass, pinned and labeled and sprayed
with preservatives. Shiny exoskeleton,
scraggly clawed legs and hideous feelers
splayed and frozen for all time.
Would you dare hold it? the kid asks
and you grimace, illustrating your answer
with an exaggerated shiver.

I wanted to lean down and whisper
into your ear how easy it is to hold
that big ugly beetle in your loose fist
letting it tickle your palm:
the trick is to not squeeze,
to not mind its ugliness
and the smell it will leave on your palm.
It's the same trick to holding my hand.

Travelogue
(for Greg)

I want to make love to you
in 15 hotel rooms
            in 14 cities.
I want to wake with the infant delight
of finding your body held
between two freshly laundered white sheets,
lightly perfumed by the smell
of these hotel room staples.

         In this room, available
to all with an open and ready wallet,
where hundreds, perhaps thousands,
      have wandered through,
& in this bed,
where hundreds, perhaps thousands,
    have slept, have made love in —
some frenzied & violent:
the spread kicked to the floor,
the sheets entangled in sweating limbs;
others clean & calm:
everything folded away neatly,
every act wiped away with hand towels.
I will know that in this one night,
this container of the temporary,
this Tupperware of wanderlust
will know what it means to be stained
with the fragments of the ghost of my craving
as it flits from one more room,
one more city, one more hotel with you.
We'll move as early pioneers did.
Wholly uncertain of what lay ahead
but heart-pounding anticipating
a pool of clear water to cleanse and quench,
a goodness, a feasting,
a soft place to lay heads,
               rest bodies.

Once I had this daydream.
We were traveling together in Tibet.
I wondered what it would be like
to kiss you in a light December Tibetan drizzle.
How the thunder would grumble in
a strange tongue, how the trees would smell
different,
            the air different.

& amidst all this foreignness,
      I would realize
the shocking familiarity of your kiss.
I would know what you taste like
even as jasmine and saffron melt on my tongue,
& as patchouli burners cloud my nose.
I would hold you to my mouth and say,
            *This is the first
            of a million kisses.*

            Come,
take it from me.

The Only Living Man In The World
(for David)

In a world where every act must
be named and where every act has
no consequences, I can take
my man in my arms and smooch him
under the stars in the fog on top
of a hill overlooking the night lights
of the city in which I love him
and call it a flowered cactus.
        He can tie me up and spit on me
in the act of lovemaking and I
will call it a yellow pearl. We
can devour all-you-can-eat rib dinners
all weekend and call it the drone of velvet.
We can delight in our isolation;
we can dodge the pinge of guilt or shame
or fear or boredom; we can be lovers
who return to a world to find friends
long gone, our homes burned to the ground,
our pets eaten, our families emigrated
to unpronounceable lands; we can burn
into each other's psyche like a brand
on the butt of a prized steer, we can get
high pissed drunk stay up all night
and get stinky in each other's arms
and I will call it the reckless
hiss of our life together.

        I tell you that if you should leave me,
my heart will turn to deep sleep and somewhere
I shall dream of acts that I cannot name
but in the darkness of my heart and I shall
invent a language that sneaks your familiar,
your cherished body into the thorny terrain
of my blood. I will talk to barbed wire
and it will talk back to me.

Nervous Days

Chinese Restaurant

I thought you'd like to know what really goes on in the kitchens of Chinese restaurants.

Well, when they say, "No M.S.G.," they're lying. When they say, "Tell us how hot & spicy," they really don't give a flying lizard fuck what you tell them, there's only one recipe, and you're going to eat it. And yes, they do spit into the food of the idiot, you know the one who everybody in the restaurant can hear: "How hot and spicy is that? Is it hot hot, or spicy hot, or chili hot, or garlic hot? It's not peppers, it is? Cos if it's too hot, I get a burning in my asshole when I shit." (Order the fucking steamed vegetables, buddy.) And yes, they do laugh quite unmercifully at the fool who actually tries to follow the pictorial instructions on how to use chopstick that's printed on the back of the chopstick wrapper. And just what the hell is Kung Pao, anyway?

In the kitchen of a Chinese restaurant they don't wash their hands much, but you already knew that. In the kitchen of a Chinese restaurant, someone is working way too hard for minimum wage but hey — it's a family thing, so it's okay and hey — it's America, where you make it if you work 12 hours a day, 7 days a week, so you can dream that American Dream, you know the one: where Diane Parkinson of *The Price Is Right* or Bob Barker of *The Price Is Right* spread it just for you. (Which one depends on your sexual orientation, No Substitutions Please. Unless, of course, you're Bi, then it's your lucky day.) Come On Down!

In the kitchen of a Chinese restaurant the waiter lives in fear of deportation, the dishwasher lives in fear of being bashed for stealing some stinking job nobody wants, the kitchen helper is scared to death of participating in the democratic political process & the chef knows someone who has AIDS at home or abroad.

From the kitchen of a Chinese restaurant I look for some semblance of the familiar. I look for home in every bite. In the dead spit of morning, after equal hours of "Silence=Death," "ACT-UP FIGHT BACK" & "What Do We Want? A Cure! When Do We Want It? Now!" I want some friendly solace & all I find is a lousy jerk-off, interrupted only by the 300-pound clerk who sticks his head through the door every ten minutes to yell, "Buy your tokens. Get into a booth or get out of here!"

I find no simple gesture can erase it all. I find a border that I cross each day for a decent wage of self-deception: call it optimism, call it a punch-fuck, fist-fucking the ass of the quality of life (and it's a tight one too, baby.)

I find a pissant pleasure, a memoir of failure, cancer for brains. & I want to go, got to go, got to find this thing called home.

In the kitchen of a Chinese restaurant, I am queer for queer & I refuse to pass my ugliness for roses. I refuse to trade my queer for your queer.

At this point you're probably thinking, wait a minute, all of this wasn't in *The Joy Luck Club*; all this wasn't in the PBS special presentation, *A Thousand Pieces of Gold*, & all of this probably isn't in that stage production of *The Woman Warrior*, either.

But I just thought that you should know what goes on in the kitchens of Chinese restaurants.

Now go eat.

Why He Had To Go

First of all, I could never get a straight answer. I'd ask, what day is it today? He'd say something like, "Everyday with you is the Summer of Love." He said it with all seriousness and sincerity which I try to replicate now but it just makes my face hurt.

Why he had to go is a mystery. Some say it was because of UFOs, the gravitational pull of Mercury in retrograde or those incurable boils on his dick.

It could be because his mother said so, his wife said so, his other lover said so, 'the voices' told him to, because all good things come to an end and we're at the Dumbo Yellow section of the parking lot waving a fond farewell to the Magic Kingdom, the Happiest Place On Earth.

Maybe it was because I wanted to fuck with those Mickey Mouse ears on. Maybe I shouldn't have told him I wanted to do those four things that I haven't done in five positions.

Maybe that Tony Robbins seminar he took triggered it. 'Ask Isadora' thinks it might be the pre-mid-life crisis or the parole violations, we need to communicate she said, and she's got a book and tape that just might help.

I'm told he had to go because he had to find himself, that he took too many pills, drank too much & refused to share any of it, because he bought a bandana for his dog at the street fair, and he shaved his balls obsessively, more so than any man should.

He had to go and now he's gone, and friends say, *You're better off without him. It's his loss. If you love somebody, let him go... There are other fish on the bus.* But all I want to do is lie in the dark with my Roberta Flack records, just me, Roberta, a grand piano and her giant afro, plotting how to destroy his property, rip his piercings out and give him herpes all because he had to go and I wanted to go first.

Buffed Fag

I want to be a buffed fag.

When I walk down the street I want folks to do a double take, gawk in disbelief, mouths agape, and say, "Oh my god! That faggot is so buffed!"

I'll spend six hours in the gym every day, blasting my quads, doing leg lifts, squats and presses and curls so I will be The Buffed Fag Of Your Dreams. I will pose and flex my muscles while having sex because that's what turns the boys on. I will have them worship my muscles and tell me how good I look as they chow down on my glutes. I'll bench press until I look like the Tazmanian Devil of Bugs Bunny cartoons, as I walk down the street in all my big chest skinny waist top heavy neanderthal arm drag swagger, thinking I'm the hottest shit in the universe and I am...

Because I am a Buffed Fag (at least I want to be). I will have sex with the towel boy at Muscle Systems, the guy who makes the protein shakes at Gold's, and the trainer at Market Street Gym; and I too will be able to pull off the bad fag attitude thing, previously reserved solely for store clerks at Tower Records and Video.

Oh, I do so want to be a Buffed Fag, hanging out in the locker rooms of gyms to pick up other buffed fags and to score injectable steroids, remembering to wash my needles with bleach and never sharing them, because I don't want to be a diseased fag, just a buffed fag with a dick shrunken to the size of a Vick's inhaler; but I won't care, because I am a buffed fag.

I will scan the L.L. Bean, J. Crew, and International Male catalogs and pick who I will marry; last week it was the one-piece perforated lycra jumpsuit, this week it's the low cut eazy-breathe fundoshi, next week it's the tan-thru bikini underwear, and folks will believe me as I partake of my fantasies because I'm a buffed fag and I have the god-given right to sail through the world being *just like everybody else*, to have the whole puny world owe me a living because everybody loves a Buffed Fag (even though they're assholes), and everybody listens to a buffed fag (even though they have the IQ and personality of a box of cat hair).

You know you too want to be a buffed fag, you can't help it as you watch them waddle down the street sure that folks would move out of their way, downing their protein shakes, spirulina shakes, shaking their way down into the psyche of Ooo-Ooo-Baby-Hot-Baby, boogieing on down to our little techno-trance dance clubs breeding ground display cases for buffed fag bodies. So c'mon, what's stopping you? Decency? Pride? (Forget it.) A sense of self-worth? (Ha.) Intelligence? A semblance of a life? (Forget that). Let's all be Buffed Fags and the whole damn scrawny world will belong to us.

Back When I Knew Who I Was

i was content to spend my afternoons
wondering what co-dependant meant
not realizing that those lazy
humid daylight hours was better
spent figuring out the physics
of dependency and codeine dreams

back when i knew who i was
i was much better than i ever thought i was
i could conjugate fuck like nobody's business
    fuck me, fuck you, fuck it, fuck him, fuck her
    fuck them, fuck yourself, holy fuck, goddamnfuckit
i could shovel dead pets off the driveway
    that my aunt ran over on her way to choir practice
    and not shed a single tear
i could choke down every family fight about money,
every caning that would come for no reason after those fights,
every time we were forced to go to my rich relatives for dinner and we'd
find ourselves in the kitchen cooking and doing the dishes.

i believed i knew the meaning of alcohol
i believed i knew how to get out of every single scrap
i believed i wasn't gonna make 25
i believed in 18 molecules of carbon
21 molecules of hydrogen
3 oxygen and one fab nitrogen
all in a sweet mixture enough to make me
feel like jennifer beals in *flashdance*
twirling my ass
in front of the snotty audition,
praying for a stinking place in
the dance-a-thon of actuality

back when my balls were the size of brazil
and my ego was the size of the antarctica
and my courage was the size of phlegm
i learned to trust few people
learned to want little
and to need even less

i learned to say "FUCK IT"
with such ease and venom
the most cynical rattlesnake
would have its underbelly turn emerald
in two seconds flat.

you could wake to find yourself in some sweet danger,
in some piss-flavored version of addiction
designed to make up for lost time,
lost ideals, lost lovers, lost causes, lost saviours
but -shit- these days,
all i find is myself back when i was
back in the conga-line of perpetual desire
the territory of an incessant need
i crave my one habit of a good man
and i want to secede from
the grip of addiction philosophy,
from the colony of "i should've known better"

fuck that 12-step thing, i say,
i like to keep my options open
and i like having the option
to get absolutely fucked up
when i feel like it,
and not feel like i fucked up, dammit.

do things change that much?
can some stupid sign from the almighty
whip you right around?
maybe i should be looking for visions of jesus
in billboards of spaghetti sauce,
visions of buddha in men's semen,
maybe i'll be a much better person
if i knew who i was when i knew who i was
but who the fuck do i think i am?
i can't even piss straight into the bowl,
can't even tell my lover that i want to cook him
breakfast for the rest of my life,
can't even cross against the light,
        (ooh walk to the light, walk to the light...)
can't pay my bills on time nor balance my checkbook

can't dance, can't mosh,
can't get fucked up like i used to, not that i want to anyway
can't take it like a man, whatever that means.

all i can is kiss who i was
back when i knew who i was
goodbye, one great big tongue smooch
and wish him a good journey
as he walks to the light
and falls off the edge of earth
and into a peaceful hell.

I'll meet up with him later.

Phone Sex

And on the 15th day God invented phone sex.

Once, just once, I was sick of being 5'10", 185 pounds, muscular, works out, blond hair, blue eyes, 8 and a half, 6 around, cut with low hanging hairy balls ready to pound your ass and fuck your face.

Once, just once, I was 5'5", 120 pounds, skinny, shaved head, tattoos, piercings, regular Masters & Johnson's 6 (depending on where you start measuring from) and the accent is because I'm a goddamn faggot chink ready to sniff your pits and wrestle you for what you want.

And the fucker hung up on me.

I'll be the first to admit that I'm not the best phone-sex fuck, something about the left brain thing. Had this guy on the phone once and the scene was asphyxiation. He said he had a plastic bag over his head and wanted me to get him off before he choked to death, and I said, "Wait a minute, how the hell can you talk on the phone if you have a plastic bag over your head? Wouldn't it get in the way of the receiver?"

And the fucker hung up on me.

So it's back to lying like mad which is the only reason why anyone has phone sex; that and possibly too much closet space filled with designer guilt neat on hangers. Let's face facts: phone sex is boring but it'll do in a snap and it *is* the great equalizer. Fucking in cyberspace, everyone stands a chance, depending on your vocabulary. (Once, some guy used the words "discombobulate" and "phallic signifier" in our smut talk, I came almost instantly.)

Once, just once, I broke the cardinal rule of Phone Sex: never meet up with who you're talking to. Packing a good knife, I went over to his place (because I didn't want him to know where I lived) and we discovered what utter fucking liars we both were. But we were horny, it was late and after two lines apiece of the crudest shit, much like snorting crushed expired aspirin, our dicks were shriveled up beyond belief with no amount of lying able to get them out of their schmoo-like flaccidity. What sheer fun.

But Phone Sex need not be dismal. Like all things, there's a way to enjoy Phone Sex as much as eating waffles in the dark. Lie like mad. Believe everything the voice on the line tells you. Choose if you want to play along with the sick fucks. Know that the other person needs it as bad as you. Know that you have nothing better to do. Know that desperation and boredom can lead to the warm belly of acceptance if you're lucky or if you fake it good. Promise everything of your body. Promise falsehood, nothing true. But most of all, reach out and touch someone and maybe someone somewhere will even switch you back and forth for free.

Lick My Butt

Lick the dry shit out of my sweaty buttcheeks

I've had my hepatitis shots so it's okay

Lick my butt
cos I'm an angry ethnic fag
& I'm in so much pain
so lick my butt

& the next time
when there's a multicultural extravaganza
& I'm asked for referrals
I can say
       "I know this guy,
       he's really cool,
       he licked my butt."

Lick my butt & tell me about
Michel Foucault's theories of deconstruction
& how it applies to popular culture,
a depressed economy & this overwhelming
tide of alienation.

Lick my butt from the center to the margins
& all the way back again.

Read Noam Chomsky in bed to me & lick my butt.

Lick my butt & give me my Prozac.
Lick my butt & call your mother, she misses you.
Flea-dip the cat & lick my butt.
Recycle & lick my butt.

Lick my butt like you really mean it.
Don't just put your tongue there
because you think it's something you should do
Do it cos you really really want to lick my butt.

My butt didn't always liked to be licked;

on the contrary, it hated anything wet
and sloppy, poking blindly
at its puckered dour grimace.
All it wanted was a nice pat,
an occasional squeeze,
a good warm seat and snug underwear.

It was happy with those,
but then all those other butts started
crashing in on its turf,
on the sidewalks and under my bed,
there were all these butts that said,
        no, demanded,
LICK ME.
My butt got tired of all that shit
& it just had to see what the fuss was all about.

At first it approached
the licking with extreme caution,
making sure all the checks
& balances were clearly present.

Hey — my butt had ever reason to be careful
it knows where it's been;
it's had enough of this bigotry
& poverty & violence
it's been on the wrong end of muggings & bashings
it's been working like a damn dog for years to make ends meet
it's been on the lam, on the block, on the contrary
& on sale for far too long

        so when that first slobber, smack,
slurp found its way into that
crack & up that uptight little asshole
it was like the Gay Pride Parade,
the Ice Capades, the Macy's Thanksgiving Day Parade
and Christmas happening all at once.

Now when I walk down the street
and you see me smiling
it's because I'm imagining

your tongue nestled in my buttcheeks
flicking away like a lizard
in a mad tweak.

Lick my butt & I'll lick yours;
we'll deal with shit of the world later.

Itchy

I want to make love to you on a bed of autumn leaves. I want to run naked in a rainstorm around an old-growth redwood with you. I want to live in a low-lying rainforest with you for five days.

But goddammit, nature makes me itchy.

Ten minutes in Golden Gate Park and I want my extra strength hydrocortisone cream.

Knowing that nature makes me oh-so itchy, the cosmic finger-fuck that is called life decided for a period in my life to let me date a series of men who were, by no stretch of the imagination, evil hippie-vegetarian-crunchies. I should have known better. The half-patchouli/half-sandalwood oil should have clued me off. The carrot-raisin-granola-tofu-roundie casserole surprise should have clued me off. The bits of dirt under his fingernails and under his reconstructed foreskin should have clued me off.

Yes, I should have known better. I should have exercised that thing of human nature known to befall humans: the ability to say "no". But they were so damn cute in their earthy unwashed hippieness and I thought, what the heck, *I'm in California. It is my destiny.*

Nature makes me itchy: I'm the guy that is on the Yosemite trail screeching, "Where's the fucking concession stand?" I'm the one who goes to the park and is psychologically allergic to grass. I think all animals, except my cat, are out to overthrow the humans and enslave us in their evil workcamps, forcing us to make chewtoys and friskies for their entertainment.

My life with evil hippies taught me things:

I learned to say with a straight face, "Yes, I love the spiritualness of this place." That will get you by in so many situations, like the DMV, cousins' weddings, strip bars, and Vegas. I learned what roughage can do for one's colon & I learned to like, hell, even appreciate all that annoying country-folky-rock music stuff. (Though I draw the line at Janis Ian, she's just way too freaky, by any means.)

The last crunchy I dated signalled the pitiful end of that period for me. Let's go rock-climbing, he said. I said, Can we just have coffee? We went to his place. He showed me his tub of endangered California yellow-striped turtles. He had a license from the state to raise these endangered little reptiles. I was supposed to watch the turtles while he went downstairs to check his chinese herbs boiling. And I just want to say: I just didn't know turtles could move that fast. And it really wasn't my fault that Martin fell off the second floor landing. Martin was in hot pursuit of Stephanie, the turtle with a full shell and distinctive markings. Rather like a Road Runner cartoon, Stephanie stepped out of the way at the last minute and true to cartoon fashion, poor lustful Martin took the cruel plunge. I rushed downstairs, picked the shell off the floor and tossed it back into the tub. I declined his invitation to go hang-gliding and camping.

Nature makes me itchy.

I like it in small small small doses. Like when I'm channel surfing and I hit a Discovery nature documentary. It's not that I don't support all those environmentally progressive things. And it's not that I don't recycle with a vengeance, a Virgo passion, so I'm told. I just think that nature is best left to those who want to deal with the unidentifiable bugs, flying or not, the omigawd-is-that-poisonous-or-not plants, the bites and salves and calamine lotion.

I'm a city kid. Give me smog, I'll call it fog. Give me the synthetic fibers and industrial culture. Give me the clank and grind of the underground. The open-all-night pageantry of freaks and clowns. Give me some pavement to plant my feet on and I'll walk you to the ends of this green Earth.

Eurodisco

In the queer '80s we were told: Feel No Guilt In Your Desires. But it's not as easy as that. I'm in a confessing sort of mood. When I'm alone at home, and I'm sure my roommate isn't going to come home anytime soon and I'm feeling a certain way, I'll pull down the shades, then I'll put on my headphones, my walkman and listen to Eurodisco at a less than prudent volume. Sometimes, I might even get off the futon and, I'm sorry, shake my ass.

I try to rationalize it. I try to say, "Well, if you *really* think about it, it's all relative. Eurodisco is really the punk equivalent of dance music. Every record seems to have been made by a couple of Dutch or Germans with a small Casio keyboard, a demon drum machine, and a skanky discobunny on way too much speed. It's as if no dance record existed before nor do they care even if they did. It's so full of that devil-may-care anarchic spirit. And those lyrics, so angst-filled. All about endless nights of displaced love, wow."

I try to say, "Fuck it, it's my life, I'm an adult, I can make my own decisions. I don't have to apologize for anything." Sometimes, I might be really intellectual about it, say, "I am not essentialist. I can fully embrace the whole sphere of audio culture."

Or I might even say, "I've listen to that damn Tribe 8 CD enough times already. One small spin of Whigfield, a few cuts of that new Bananarama remixed CD won't hurt."

But I just want you to know that I don't have a problem, I can stop anytime I want.

Some people say my secret disco fixation is a transition thing, that it can lead to worse vices. But I don't believe that. The other day on *Oprah*, a psychologist said that cigarettes and alcohol can lead to hard drugs and pornography. Well, I skipped straight to pornography, so I am what is known as a non-transitional type personality. And even if I was a transitional type personality, what could Eurodisco lead to? In the worse case scenario, I might develop a dire need to buy expensive designer clothes and hang out at dance clubs where others just like me gather for mutual support. (Yes, there are others that share this aural orientation too, you know.) I might spend all week waiting for Friday night so I can be with others like me. Spend five hours getting ready, missing the 12 a.m. departure time, ending up in a smoky dance club at 2:01 a.m. picking up some queen and having meaningless unfulfilled and utterly boring vanilla sex where I'd probably catch a bad case of herpes and anal warts (or worse), thus dashing all dreams of being "Butt of the Month" in *Advocate Men*, filling me with so much despair and bitterness that I'd commit suicide by driving a Toyota hatchback filled with explosives into the display window of Headlines or Rolo or All-American-Boy in the Castro.

But that's the worse case scenario, and the chances of that happening are really quite slim. After all, I can't drive.

So, I might even say, "Some cool people have bad Eurodisco records. Eartha Kitt is one of the coolest people alive and she made two tacky Eurodisco records."

And my orientation is to *Euro*disco specifically, not the generic North American brand, and not the Asian or South American knock-offs, though they are pretty cool too. (I concede that Australia is an unknown faction.)

But I just want you to know that I only do it recreationally and it's controlled. It's not like I secretly dash off to Sam Goody's in Milpitas to buy so that no one will recognize me. I can stop anytime I want, but I just like the sense of it. Come by sometime, and maybe I'll save a taste from you.

These Nervous Days

These nervous days,
I want to kiss you. I want to just kiss you & hold you. I want to kiss you & hold you & hug you & love you & kill you. I want to kick my habit. I want to open a border & close a bank. I want to open a mind & close a heart. I want to open a shopping center & close a stadium. I want to have my own talk show. Yeah I want a low-fat low-cholesterol guilt-free snack (cos I've got a yummy yummy in my tummy tummy). I want a new gas mask. I want to be the other white meat. I want to Deal-A-Meal. I want better weapons than you. I want to kill more people than you. I want fuck more people than you. I want to fuck over more people than you. I want better nipples. I want my say even if I've got nothing to say. I want your new-age ritualistic karma fuck-me-all. I want to kick your habit. I want to make you love me like you love your dog. I want to meet Traci Lords and ask her why. I want to meet Jeff Stryker and tell him to stop it. I want to be a buffed fag. I want to discriminate against more people than you. I want to spread my brand of hate-filled ideology with more venom than you. I want to spread more love than your Mama. I want to know who's on first and why the fuck is he on first and not me, dammit. I want to lick you butt, spread your asscheeks and lick the dry shit out of your sweaty butthole. I want to swallow. I want to be the last victim of cynicism, crucified on the cross of Fuck-You. I want to be the first one to tell you.

And in these nervous days,
I want you to give me yr money. Give me yr spare change. Give me five. Give me a break. Give me a better gig. Give me a minute. Give me a lifetime. Give me yr mantra. Give me yr American history. Give me my American history. Give me (gimme gimme) a man after midnight, won't somebody help me chase the shadows away. Give me yr firstborn. Give me a hand. Give me just a little more time. Give me God in a teacup. Give me God in a toilet duck. Give me yr underpaid underemployed job. Give me this all ages show. Give me a stiff drink. Give me a good beer. Give me hope. Give me the serenity to accept the things I cannot change, the courage —oh fuck that shit—. Give me shelter. Give me another chance, it's never happened before, I was just tired. Give me another chance, I'm sorry I won't do that ever again. Give me some cheap sentiment. Give me some sweet pain. Give me some chicken tonight. Give me your tired, your weary, your huddled masses

yearning to breathe free. Give me yr cum, yr piss, yr spit. Give me yr infected blood. Give me yr diseased genitals. Give me yr STDs. Give me yr best make-up tips. Give me yr secrets to clear skin, beauty, success & weight loss. Give me more power Scotty. Give me some sense of empowerment. Give me some sense of security. Give me yr best shot. Give me yr stinking crown. Give me more. Give me.

Give me what I ask for & you can take what you want from me.

Smooch

Growing up in a Muslim country, where the TV programs imported from the evil west were scrupulously snipped by the censor's eager scissors to protect the goggle-eyed masses from the prophet of lust: the kiss. Presumably, watching too many unmarried kisses or too passionate a married kiss on that flickering light box would somehow inflame one's loins to all sorts of sinful deeds and unwanted pregnancies and moral decay.

Only last week, I realized that I watched a full year of *The Love Boat* without ever seeing anyone kiss. The two lovers would approach, eyed closed harlequin romance style, lips puckered, background muzak full throttle, and a bad disjointed edit later, the two would be seen pulling away with that satisfied look of PG-13 fulfillment.

In retrospect, the only kiss that I wanted to have seen was Vicki Stubbing's first kiss.

Vicki Stubbing, the captain's chubby daughter played by Jill Whelan, was such a monstrous pleasure. She was hideous in that unredeeming way, and once she hit puberty, the producers took great pains to assert her new found breasts and hormonal imbalances. Vicki had to start falling in love with guest stars every other week:

Vicki loves Dack Rambo but he's in love with Michelle Lee.

Vicki loves Parker Stevenson but he's in love with Pamela Sue Martin.

Vicki loves James Farentino but he's in love with Charo, for the third time this month.

After the third commercial, Vicki would witness the object of her affection pull away from the said bimbette with puckered lips. Then good Captain Stubbing, lead on a tip by Gopher, would find her weeping in a mascara-drip in a deck chair and there would be the requisite moonlit "Vicki-when-you-get-old-enough-you'll-meet-a-very-special-man-who-will-be-so-lucky" speech.

Eventually, Vicki managed to get her kiss (Willie Aames), one that wasn't brotherly or fraternal but heck, that wasn't spared by the censors either.

No kiss was spared: Not Joanie and Chachi, not *Knightrider*, not Dirk Benedict in the A-Team, not the entire *The Facts of Life*, not JR Ewing, not Mr. and Mrs. Hart to Hart.

For a while, I always wondered what it would be like to be a passenger on the Love Boat, how exciting to be filled with all sorts of wacky adventures and romantic twists and to finally get that forbidden kiss. But by then

I was already kissing old men in restrooms of shopping malls. Old men who were grateful for any decent grope they could get their hands on while their wives and children ran amok shopping, oblivious. They would sit on the toilet bowl, put me on their laps, and rub up against me in a mixture of forbidden pleasure and fear that the security guards might burst in at any moment.

And I sat there in stall after stall trying to reconcile the smell of old men's gums and the Love Boat philosophy of life pocketing whatever small gifts of cash they gave me in exchange for that one brief moment of young cum.

Eventually, we got caught. One unfortunate old guy who had the displeasure of moaning too loudly got us busted, but I managed to pretend that he forced me into the stall and as the security guards let me go with his watch and his $40 still in my pocket, I saw in that old guy's eye a look that has stayed with me from toilet stalls to back rooms, adult bookstores and bathhouses.

The Love Boat philosophy has served me well:

In the space of that bad edit, seen only by a religious zealot with scissors and by your imagination, that apparent kiss can mean anything, it can lead to anything and it can mean nothing but a means to fill a space.

The Love Boat got cancelled, half the cast were on drugs and were continually doped up throughout the last few seasons. One ran for Congress, one became a housewife, one started his own business, one got totally washed-up, and I figured out how to smooch boys the right way.

Ex-Boyfriends Named Michael

My mother is concerned that I haven't met a nice boy to settle down with. She keeps asking me if I've met the right guy yet.

Well, Mom, there've been some nice guys who just didn't work out, some guys that have broken my heart, and there've been ex-boyfriends named Michael.

Ex-boyfriend named Michael #1 was a sheer mistake, but we make such delightful mistakes when we are young. You're supposed to learn from your mistakes, but heck...

Ex-boyfriend named Michael #2. I've washed him right out of my colon. Just for once, I'd like to date a man and not his therapist.

Ex-boyfriend named Michael #3 said I had communication problems, and I said, "Oh, go fuck yourself asshole." What I should have said was, "Honey, I am trying to understand your feelings of frustration at our seemingly inept articulations of our emotions, but I do have some unresolved feelings of anger towards you, so please go fuck yourself, asshole."

But maybe there's the off chance he's right. I have never been that great at communicating. Ex-boyfriend named Michael #4: I should have known better the first time we met and went back to his apartment to fuck. His idea of fuck music was Dan Fogelberg's *Greatest Hits*. I asked him to change the CD, and he changed it to the only thing that could have been worse: *Neil Diamond Live at Madison Square Garden*.

Coming to America, indeed.

But I stuck with him and every fuck at his place was sheer hell. I tried telling him that his taste in music sucked and that I could seriously help him, but somehow I lacked the communication skills to do just that. But then I thought I loved him, and then I was young enough and foolish enough to believe that love can overcome Linda Ronstadt.

It cannot.

But love did not stop me from throwing his Yanni CDs behind the bookcase nor did it stop me from torching his *Ballads of Madison County* CD on the gas stove. Oh, what a beautiful blaze it was! He swore the CD was a gift but like all ex-boyfriends named Michael, he was a lying dog. Now I'm getting ahead of myself here, that's about creatively destroying ex-boyfriends' property, not about ex-boyfriends named Michael.

Ex-boyfriend named Michael #5 was suffering from a severe case of yellow fever and dumped me for some little Taiwanese guy, fresh off the damn boat. Two weeks in the Yoo-Ass and the little pissant faggot manages to find his way to Cafe Hairdo, ready to be picked up by his American Dream of Homosexual Romance. I can just see him sitting there, legs crossed, working his non-threatening little Third World charm, offering to share his table and newspaper. I can just see them now: sharing haircare products, making mutual consensual decisions about dinner, movie, sex and their emotional well-beings. I can see them sitting on the sofa with the dictionary in their laps trying to figure out the difficult words in Barbara De Angelis' *Making Love Work* video seminar, and thinking about adopting a fox terrier named Honey. I can see them having deep, deep discussions about which one of them has a better butt:

"You do."

"You do."

"No, you do."

"Stop it! You do."

"Yours is tight and tanned."

"But your is pert and angry."

What a pair of goddamn fucking freaks. I would just like to see them in a big car accident crashing into an oncoming truck carrying a shipment of Ginzu kitchen knives.

But hey, I'm not bitter, I'm descriptive. I'm not jaded. I just have too many ex-boyfriends named Michael.

Just once, I'd like to see everything of my life with ex-boyfriends named Michael laid out on a fat barge sent off to the landfill of affection. I'll watch the barge ferry it's way through the flotsam of therapy & crabs, dishsoap & bad sex, shared shirts & worry , devotion & drugs, pissed-off nights & legless drunken revelry.

I'll wave goodbye and I'll be fine.

Home

Twelve hours from San Francisco to Tokyo/Narita. Seven hours from Toyko/Narita to Singapore. Six hour layover. One hour Singapore to Kuala Lumpur. One hour Kuala Lumpur to Kuantan and I'm home.

Just my luck to be stuck in a section filled with white Hindus from California en route to Calcutta for the Oneness Home Peace Run. Sixty white Hindus who did not preorder the Vegetarian or Hindu meal. (Why one of the young Hindus is carrying a Head tennis racket on his trip is beyond me.) My mood is soothed by watching sixty white Hindus having to watch Arnold Schwartzenegger in *True Lies*. Most of the group chose to watch without the sound, and at least two were forced to chant and/or meditate to deal with the silent violence they are subjected to at the cruising altitude of 60,000 feet. I really wanted the chicken, but when you're stuck in a plane with sixty white Hindus, you just got to have the beef. *Hmmm. Chicken with penne pasta in a tomato sauce or braised Hindu God with wild rice fiesta?*

China Airlines. All the stewardesses look like they plucked each other's eyebrows in some mad layover party in Bucharest.

Singapore International Airlines. If I ever wanted to give white people preferential treatment, I'd become an Singapore Airlines flight attendant. It's as if the Commonwealth never fell and Queen Victoria's coronation is still Number One in its timeslot.

Northwest Airlines. Grumpy fallen prom queens who keep powdering their faces to prevent oil slicks. By the time we're touching down, it looks like a Kabuki opera in full swing down the aisles.

Singapore. Home away from home. The name du jour for little boys these days is Alvin; for little girls, it's Fiona. In fifty years, Alvins and Fionas will be running the government.

Another plane, another crappy airport. Finally, home. A small fishing town that is known to Europeans for the Club Med that opened fifty miles up the coast but had to be closed most of the year because the South China Sea proved to be too rough, the undertow too brutal, and little battered sea-bloated white German tourist bodies kept floating up to shore. But Home, home on the range. My mom wants me to go to church. I tell her I will be worshiping at St. Flannel's, Our Lady of Perpetual Mattress, Head Pastor: the Rev. P. Low. She is not amused. She has been touched by the Holy Spirit. I've got to give my mom credit. She upped and left the church she had been going to for the last twenty-five years because she thought they were too conservative. She did not want to wear a veil to services. She disagreed with the elders' interpretation of the bible. Now, she's a Liberal Charismatic. She believes in gifts of the Holy Spirit, speaking in tongues and casting out demons. The other week, she tells me, Mrs. Aw started behaving strangely during service and was stuck by demons that had to be cast out. Demons may have been involved in Mrs. Aw's breast cancer and subsequent double mastectomy. Next week, they're going on a road trip to cast out a demon (or demons) in a family friend who fell mysteriously ill after moving a Buddhist shrine out of an abandoned house.

The Internet is the big buzz. Everybody wants to know if I know any good smutty sites, but all I know is the site where people talk about the things they shove up their ass. My little cousins want to know how much Doc Martins costs in the Yoo-Ass and if I can send them some. My grandmother shows me the spot where her mah-jong buddy hung herself when she couldn't stand the chemotherapy to kill the cancer in her eye. My dad shows me where the medicine men and his girlfriend killed the superstitious state legislator and buried his body under five feet of cement, where the new freeway is. The five-mile stretch of road, haunted because fifty years ago Japanese POW death camps were housed there, is now prime real estate. The Sultanate has been stripped of their political powers by a Constitutional Amendment.

A car smashed into an old shophouse and half of it collapsed in a scientific cross-section exposing an old coolie's room where he has lived for the last forty years, his extensive collection of girlie calenders and magazines collected in boxes, shelves and on walls glimmer like seeds in a cut tropical fruit. The roads have all been renamed. The market has moved. There's a new bus station. The new floating restaurant on the river sank after a week. The monsoons come late now.

I find myself where the demons of nostalgia holds me. The awkward silences. The scraping of silverware against fine china plates as childhood friends turn as familiar as first dates. The foreignness of a place where many happy teenage hours were spent. The persistent croaking of toads in the monsoon dampness. The pets in the yard changed and the new ones do not recognize and are cruel.

The sounds of revelry from the nearby holiday resorts filter in like distant windchimes, and in the dark of night, the streetlamp's burnt out again, the demons of home come fierce as a lover's kiss.

Tour

I keep telling myself that it will be the last time but it never is, and then mom starts on her, *it's just four days a year... it's for your parents... just to relax... when you were younger we didn't have money, and we were working everyday...* monologue.

And I end up on going on The Family Vacation.

Did I say vacation? Mom and Dad like tours, package tours, or Wholesale Vacations as their trusty travel agent calls it. So, for the third year in a row, I have been a member of one of those Chinese Tour Groups. The ones that travel everywhere together in the mini-bus, following the leader with the flag, heading en masse to the buffet, each wearing the tour badge for easy identification in case they get lost, probably carrying the complimentary tour bag.

Following the leader to: 1. Food. Provided, three meals a day without fail, preferably dumbed down so that it won't be too much of a dietary culture shock. 2. Cheap souvenir shopping. Keychains are big, my mother has this unnatural affinity for keychains; and 3. Zesty 'bargains' where the tour guide will guarantee its value, discount and authentic worth. Bargain, Discount, and Buffet are key words in these tour groups. Much of the tour is spent complaining incessantly about how horrible the food is and how expensive everything is. Then on the last day, we'd take a big group photo and we'd all tell each other how this was the best tour ever, and how we would recommend it to all our friends and colleagues.

This year, it's Samosir Islands, a small volcanic island and mountain resort in Indonesia. Fly to Kuala Lumpur, fly to Medan, take the tour coach to mountains, travel time: four hours. Various factories pay the tour company to drag the tourists to their shops, and so even if we are late or exhausted beyond belief, we still have to stop at the Asli shop for their Famous Peanut Candy. Peanut candy that will strip your tongue and throat of all semblance of moisture and mucus.

Our tour guide is a young lady called Elizabet. I thought it was a misspelling, a mispronunciation, but her tourist board I.D. confirms that she is indeed, *Eliza-bet*. Miss Lian to the nth degree. She spends all day talking very loudly into the bus microphone and telling us stupid crude jokes of the scatological or sexual nature. Sample: "You guess who farts louder? Men or ladies? Men, or course, because they got a microphone and two loudspeakers!" She also insists on audience participation and making us *guess-*

lah. Sample: "You know when Indonesia's Independence Day is? You guess lah!" "You know how to tell if your money is real or not? You guess lah! Okay, take the 10,000 Rupiah note, that one got a picture of a man on it but it's not my father because he's so ugly. You guess is who!" Elizabet is a low-rent Anita Mui knock-off. She has the kind of look and grating voice that only Cantonese men from Hong Kong can find appealing. It takes her a full day before she realizes that half the tour bus doesn't even speak English, not even the broken half-constructed pidgin dialect English that she speaks and her piquant scatological wit had been wasted for a full day. Incidentally, the picture on the note was of the Sultan and the test for counterfeit notes was merely another of her merry repartee: she made the tour bus fold the note very tightly then to open the crumpled note to check that the Sultan's spectacles had not been crushed. How we laughed.

By the time we reach the jetty, half the bus is drunk on the cheap Bintang beer, and the other half have had their throats sandpapered from the Famous Peanut Candy. And it's still an hour by the little ferry travelling at half a knot per hour to the little island resort. I'm amazed at my brother's ability to fall asleep at any time and at any place.

The hotel resort is not what it looks like in the brochure. The plastic wrap is still on the furniture that is falling apart. Just our luck to arrive in the middle of dog-mating season, and all night we sleep with the yelping and howling of mangy doggies fucking. I can hear my parents complaining through the thin walls. I can hear my parents making out through the thin walls.

The next morning, Mom is trying to be positive about the whole experience, after all, it's Family Time, and so she's trying to enjoy the scenery but the trees are in her way. You should cut down all those palm trees so that they won't obstruct the view from the second floor balcony, she tells the receptionist at the front desk. Mom has brought her *Reader's Digest* with her and occasionally tries to amuse us with a funny story or an Anecdote From Real Life. Dad is reading *Golf Digest*, and we all know that all in all, he would rather be teeing off somewhere. He's sitting in the shade plotting his next Senior Golfers tournament strategy, and the new microwave or fruit juicer or electric spa that he might win and never use. My brother is trying to brief a case, calling his secretary long-distance to check the telex and spends a lot of time sleeping. I am counting leaves in the tree, and trying to remember all those novels I read about POWs and how they pass the time.

You have to understand that we all play a role in this vacation: Dad gets to play the archetypal father, provider, brings the family on vacation and protects them from things foreign. Mom gets to be the archetypal mother, who wants nothing more than her family together for quality time. My brother gets to play the First Son, with the good job, time away from litigating little orphans, and interesting stories about colleagues, secretaries, law school buddies and scandalous lawsuits. I get to play Goram, the ungrateful beast-child from Sodom who cannot do anything right and has absolutely no income potential.

I hate being a tourist, but at certain points of the Family Vacation, I know I just have to give up, put certain social-political convictions on hold and just go with the flow. I always say never again, but then I see how happy my folks are, the proud photos my mom frames and chucks on the mantle, and I see Dad on that one misty casino night on Vacation 1994, wrapped up in his high school reunion track suit, zippered all the way up to his neck to protect him from the cold air, holding onto the red plastic casino cup of twenty-cent coins, like a little kid clutching a mug of ribena. I see how tiny he is, how lost he looks, how innocent his bald spot, bifocals and hunched five-foot frame looks, wandering among the slot machines, the poker and blackjack tables, the gamblers and the high-rollers, and little old ladies determined to make a fortune, and I know how strong and muscular his hands were when he had to give us our inoculations, stitch up the cut above my eye, lance and drain infections on my limbs, and probe at unexplained lumps in my abdomen.

And I know that next year, I'm going to be in another buffet line, another tour bus, smiling big for endless instamatic photos.

Pisser

Cocksucker's Blues

Beauty does not come cheap
but there are enough discount stores out there.
Pennies turn to dimes,
dimes into nothing but hard time.
I walk the city with my eyes shut
against the flesh crawl of need,
ducking into alleyways and bookstores
lined with pathetic creatures begging for blow
and a buffed jock named Chad begging
for one more token, one more day
at a time. It's enough to keep
the saddest cocksucker happy.

Somewhere South of Market,

You said you used to be so beautiful
that people would pay to suck you off
and you didn't even have to cum to collect
but now you would let anyone have you
you have no choice, you said,
and I agreed and tried to make you
feel like a million bucks for $4.99.

Buy your beauty:
At 10, it tastes like spit
        at 20: melted government margarine
        at 30: Elmer's glue paste
        at 40: vaseline
don't bother going any higher,
pack your bags, and hit the road, Jack,
it'll never taste like what you paid for
no matter how high you can get.

You crowned yourself Queen of the Poppers.
Sucked so much amyl nitrate
that the vapors were the only thing
holding your tongue together,
the Tic-Tac of your dependency coats your words.
Your silk suit crumpled, your body in a cold sweat

your flaccid penis tasting like stale elbow grease
your icy balls stretched into a tight bruised blue
to match your lips that had turned turquoise hours ago.
You said, you needed a few more lines to turn it up.
Damaged goods, but who isn't these days?

In Vegas at the Mirage,
Sigfried and Roy's White Tigers trapped
in a perpetual daylight, 24 hours of fake light
in a plexiglass cage with a glittering waterfall
landscape out of The Snow Queen.
Poor tigers held up to the scrutiny
of the ugly sour-faced masses
decked in sequins, appliques and wash-and-wear,
spongy folk who have lost so much currency
shoved down metal slots.
Only impotence can drive someone
to look at tigers at 3 in the morning.

At 3 in the morning,
I follow reflections and piss-stained corridors
to bedsits and broomsticks.
The first time the first time the first time.
He was a wino a bum a banker a chemist a greengrocer.
He was a lawyer a doctor a systems analyst.
His name was Rico, he wore a diamond.
He slapped me around he fucked my face
he came in my mouth when I asked him not to.
He showed me pictures of younger boys
polaroids of bodies without heads, hands holding dicks,
fingers in asses, smooth armpits
and said I want you to be just like that.
I wanted to die when he got too mean and too rough
I wanted to kill him when he apologized
and offered a sandwich, a ride home when it was done
I wanted to swallow more, swallow more.
Maybe that wasn't the first time,
it could have been the 2nd or 3rd
it could have been every subsequent time.
It could also be nothing but a done-up jack-off lie.
Just one for my baby and one for the road.

I crawl out at dawn
into the soup of light and scarred gratitude.

A crazed Born-Again bearing a sandwich board
approaches, gives me a tract
that will save me from the evils of the material world.
Repent, he says, *repent.*
There is healing in the blood in the Lamb of Christ.

580 billion babies have died in my mouth.
580 billion more will follow, their daddies abandoning them,
like AIDS-infected darlings, in spit and in confession.
I repent nothing.

I would do much more.

I would dance barefoot on shards of your broken beauty.
I would call you Daddy in the face of my sadist master.

I would match Rod Stewart's record
12 pints and they won't have to pump it out of me,
I will choke it down and keep it down.

Ask me anything. Tell me anything.
I want all beauty to weep for me.
I wear my wounds on my tongue,
my dependency is my king,
and my immortal imperfection, my fractured wings.

Pisser

You tell me that this kiss means I'm your boy and that your lover doesn't understand your craving for young smooth boys to play dead for you, the bear of a man that he is and how you now cannot bear the sight of his face nor his body nor his cock, you need a boy to lie across your lap *tell me a secret* you whisper in my ear *tell your daddy your secrets* and I spit my spirit of transaction into your ear. This is such a fucked-up way to score but -shit- what's a person to do when your dealer changes his phone number and doesn't give it to you — you either take it personally, take it as a sign from the almighty to get clean or you improvise, easy choice when the only voice on the other end of the line plies your ear with sweet promises in some adult bookstore, yeah, desperation and dependency can make me fake it good, yeah, I can fake that virgin shit, that innocent-fuck shit, that I-haven't-had-good-sex-until-you shit, being a bespectacled chink helps & he wants to know a secret so I tell him about how my uncle buttfucked me when I was 10 which explains my daddy-fetish & *oh daddy daddy, feed me your cum daddy*

I lie like mad & he laps it up like a stray mongrel licking Sizzler throw-outs *feed your boy your cum, daddy* I whisper and he feeds me with semen, sweet greens, money, gifts, promises. Oh, he feeds me good & he feeds me like I was some starving Third World child touched by the blessed golden hand of Sally Struthers and the Christian Children's Fund & he feeds me & oh, I eat, I eat and I eat like I was that starving Third World child wide-eyed visited with the blessing of All-You-Can-Eat, every meal was like the last meal on death-row, belly full & I shat the whole day to keep up with my feeding schedule & I ate till I puked until I kissed sweet sleep.

But like the well-fed, contented with my buddha-belly filled with yummy treats, hips swelling fat, I learned to give it away for free. I thought I found my 24-hour open-all-night 7-11 of satiation, yeah, I gave it away, I thought I found the high road to all that I couldn't bear, every wisp of grief that I couldn't bear, my heart, my lungs, my liver, my guts, my eyes, my ears, my heart.

I give it away all the time and I also take too much but damn the buffet table doesn't go on forever, nothing ever does & he moves on to some little Latino kid who satisfies him better than I could.

I see you through the glory hole at the adult bookstore, you have him in the black sheer crotchless panties that you once offered to put me in. He is sitting on your lap, you are masturbating with one hand, one hand free to feed the tokens, he is curled on your lap, your head is buried in his skinny chest, he is curled silent as an aborted foetus and you are stroking him and cooing like a pigeon on speed. I do not notice that I am kneeling in a pool of someone else's cum. After you leave, I sit on the small stool and bring my knee up to my mouth and suck at the fluid in the fabric, sucking out someone else's cum that I say is yours, that you put your dick through the hole and left your cum just for me and now I am feeding on it like a hungry mosquito, like a baby hungry for a spurt of teat milk.

But nothing goes on forever, not that craving for some consecrated high in slosh & grind, not for anonymous cum, nothing goes on forever but this bursting in my chest, this new addiction that I hold in my ribs, this bursting, this little pisser desire, this queer desire, I take a swig of my heart and baby, lean in, let me tell you one last secret. If I were to leave my body and never come back to it, if I were to leave my blood and never again taste the metal of it, if I were to leave my semen in some stranger's rectum, leave my brain in some discarded pool of my past, leave my desire in the scarred light of damaged goods and benevolent memories, I will know that in the crux of any reckoning, this queer desire defines a locus wider, more than where my dick has been and who it has regretted.

Why A Boy

In the dark room, lit only by the a stray light from a bathroom somewhere in the back of the house and the blue emanation of porn from the television, the joint is passed back and forth. The drill sergeant is stuffing a dripping fat dildo into the recruit's ass, the sound is turned so low that each thrust, each play-acting wince on the boy's face sounds like a whisper in a great library. The actors rarely ejaculate on this tape and soon it runs out, follows the stains up the wall to the ceiling, spatter of crisco and shit, some homeowners stick little luminous stars on their ceilings so that they can gaze at the heavens as they lay on the floor, but heaven means different things to different people and he changes the tape. Another fister. I ask him what was the biggest thing he ever had up his ass. He scratches his bread, smooths the hairs over his balding head and thinks. I wish he would say something really fantastic like, "A watermelon," or "Half a cocker spaniel," but he says, "Two hands."

"Some people got bigger hands," he says, "and two hands at the same time is much bigger than a foot." The joint is done, the lines are done and the action on the television guides us. With my arm in his ass, I feel the rough nubs of his vertebrae. I wriggle my fingers and see how they pop up against his old belly, feel the twist-tie of his belly button from the inside. I look down and creeping out of his ass, plugged by my arm, a thin stream of blood, red as all of last year's misery, flows. *Who's a daddy?*

I put off visiting and when I finally do see him, it's not as bad because he's put back on the weight he lost months ago and they changed his medication and so he's not so spaced out anymore. Soon, someone will have to take care of him all day and all of the night, and across the world in a Buddhist hospice in Bangkok, what's left of a man tries to sleep. The only comfort he has is the picture of his teacher. Next week, he will be left to die in a hospital because someone will bomb the place. Next week, a Man will find a Boy and take him to his heart and home and cock and wallet, and the Boy will find something in that. *Who's a boy?*

The phone rings and I agree to meet him because his wife is away for the day. He says he imagines if I were his little boy neighbor who would worship his cock everyday, drink off his balls. Once in a park, a bus station, a dead end, a man told me he had a friend in Santa Cruz who picked up street kids so he could rub some crank in their asses and pump the boy silly. Let's visit him sometime, he said, and I never saw him again, and maybe somewhere in this wide country a boy is really being fucked by his daddy's crystal smeared dickhead.

What a daddy, what a boy wants is an unspoken agreement that parents should never ever have to bury their children. Tonight I can't sleep and my eyes are too tired to read and the voice on the television is hysterical ranting about how fathers are missing in our culture, how men don't take responsibilities anymore, how role models are missing, how homosexuality is threatening the family which is already threatened because there are no men, not enough men. Once many years ago, we danced to a proclamation that there were too many men and way too little time. It used to rain men, godammit. Oh prophesy that is disco, tell us where we can find the love to love ya baby, let's just blame it on the boogie.

When a daddy, when a boy finds that everyone around me seems to be dying and I wonder if I'm not too. Seems the whole world is dying and the speed of surviving, existing here now is waiting for that final impact, that head-on collision, the shock that may or may not break your neck. Look over here, in Goya's suite *Disasters of War*, the 81st etching shows us the Proud Monster, a horrible beast whose regurgitating maw pours out an avalanche of men. Oh, my Terrible Father devours me. I want to be the hero in my own version of this story but I am too often the monster, puking out my share of fathers, grandfathers, brothers, uncles, cousins, nephews, sons, grandsons, contributing to the shortage and it feels like sitting in a pool of blood like hunting for God's cum like watching the whole world spin like a teacup ride at Disneyland like knowing why a daddy and, if you're still here in the sound of my voice, know why a boy.

Postcard Angels
(in memory of Donald Brown)

I.
Tell me what it is.
Tell me what it's like.

II.
Infected.
Blotting the crisp clean white
sheets with my poisoned blood. Poison
that flows through my arteries, my veins,
into my major organs, my brain, taking over
my body. It is a wound untaken care of
and the germs get drunk
on my blood, collapsing, infecting.

Lying with codeine and fried chicken to comfort
me and miles of sterile gauze. I pull
the strip of gauze plugging my wound out,
one foot long and still coming, still
dripping, with pus - dried and fresh,
and blood - dried and fresh, draping
over my hands like christmas tree tinsel,
like the intestines of a chicken,
freshly slaughtered.

III.
Tell me what pain is. A child
forced to go to Sunday School with bruises
and scars on his face beaten by an irate aunt.
When I fell off my bicycle and cut myself bad,
I was scolded for crying. I found out
that I had "a low threshold of pain" and that
I should be thankful I "don't have to give birth."

Two hours in the dentist chair with a man
face half covered in green, hanging
over me, working at chiseling, chipping,
digging to get a tooth out and blood
vaporizing, splattering, all reflected

in his thick glasses. At least
there is no pain. Blessed Novocaine.

IV.
Is it standing long hours in some steam room,
standing in dark corners of bathhouses,
waiting in a park on some cold night,
waiting beside my glory hole in some stinking john,
waiting for somebody to give me the warmth
of a body pressed so close against mine,
waiting for the reassurance of a cock
thrust at my waiting lips
to tell me that I am still here
and still alive to burst the stitches
in my mouth because I couldn't wait
for a week before sucking cock?

Is it the next morning
being sick to my stomach
wondering who the fuck fucked who
and whether the man lying beside me
knows anyone I know and wondering whether
he will come back to haunt me later?

V.
That feeling that fills me when I am sipping Coke
and eating my bowl of chili while the sun laps
at my being three hours after the phone call of another
who has slipped back to the comforts of booze
and cheap dope because the bomb in his blood
exploded too soon, poisoning, infecting.

Is it pain when he laughs that deep laugh
so deep that it cannot be filled with anything?

Is it pain when I realize that
he planted the time of his blood,
of his cum, right in my ass,
shot right in like a hypodermic needle
shooting up?

VI.
Pain is an eyesore sitting
in a twenty-four hour diner drinking
cups of tepid coffee realizing
that two decades is not even a life,
that cannot sleep without dreaming
of a fantasy with no pain.

Two hours, and the cheap coffee will mix
with the alcohol and gastric juices,
a sweet cocktail that, like mother's milk,
will lull me to sleep.

VII.
Tell me what pain is in dreams.
Do angels fly out of postcards
and kiss you when it hurts?
Does it ever hurt in dreams?
Can you be crucified, murdered,
tortured, hanged, burned alive,
eaten to the bone, diseased
and still find your body again?
Do we become angels in dreams,
where we shed our tired and wrecked bodies
at the door and get new outfits
and new flesh that works
like flesh is supposed to work?

Let us trade our lives, our hearts.
Let us trade tongues.
Lie beside me and let
the white stuff of our love
hold us together.
Let me sleep too, good man,
let me sleep the sleep where
10,000 angels at the foot of my bed
cannot wake me.

Chinese New Year

It is Chinese New Year and I am standing
at the corner of Broadway and Kearny
feeling the warm brush of bodies scurrying
into stores frantic, pleased
and brisk with the glow of celebration.
Soon the gleaming roast ducks,
the carefully spit-turned roasted pork ribs,
the translucent skinned chicken steamed
in sesame oil and the raw fish tossed
in lettuce, mint and peanut sauce
will grace someone's table:
a feast of richness, a wish
of prosperity, a life
of blessing.

No heads will be washed today, no houses swept
& don't think about death: it's bad
luck. I cast my numbers,
and as I age another year,
superstitions don't hold their weight
anymore than voodoo heebie-jeebie
medicinal claims.
    So come take me Year of the Monkey:
witty, articulate, passionate, youthful, vain, immature.
Make me happy with your promises
of luck and life
because it is Chinese New Year
and for a few blocks, the train
of pom pom girls, the Lowell High School band
and sequined Ms. Chinatown will pass
on the same streets where I opened my body
in the rattle of festivities, the creed
of color, the spook of flesh.

You took the uncompromising facts
of my living. Spread it out maplike
as a dangerous game. *Spy vs. Spy*
like in *MAD* magazine. You appear to me
as golden frogs. You pour rain water

from pitchers colored with familiarity over me.
I bathe in smells of palm oil, rubber
sap, cannon fodder. Fireworks
grace my feet. I put white
smoke billowing from homemade
crackers on your forehead.
Somehow this might soothe your pain
and mine. Tie ginger in sackcloth,
the tips soaked in kerosene. Suck
illness right out. Strength
nudes itself to my scrawny arms
barely able to throw a good punch
and your life starts unraveling
as mine reveals itself in
this viral flash. A 25¢ peepshow
separated by a sliding opaque
screen flashing ex-lovers,
ex-boyfriends, one night stands, blind dates
and ex-families. Tokens
fill empty jars in our respective rooms.
Candles light the stuff of our
secrets. Sometimes we lie like mad
and civility spurts
like Chinese New Year and I come
festooned with ashes and bones,
hard crumbling and all
too memorable. Miserable. Teal
pours from my mouth. Blood
of every wound, every conceivable
brilliance hides in my hair.
The hard work of walking and waking
ploughs itself in my skull
and I am ready to be brimmed
with the tasks of renewals
and burials.
I have prepared for my feasting.
I've paid my debts. I've housecleaned:
updated the address book, keeping
the names and numbers unused
anymore, written in disparate script
each, in its safe place.

The last grounding on memory must be respected.
On the day that I am nothing more
than handwriting in some trick's
book, I will return to your memory
and the hundreds of others.
I will stand in pink fog.
Cats will breathe silent over me.
Talismans will hang from my chest.
Shiny prophecies will pierce my nipples.
My flesh will be smooth as cold coffee.
I will be a haunting
that speaks across waters, borders
and peacetime.

Did I ever think I would make it this far?
Did I make it anywhere at all?

For now, let's push all that
to the back of our minds like shame,
let's wave to Ms. Chinatown,
fill our bellies with food and laughter,
entertain our guests, visitors,
families, tell stories — real
and made up, be together, make love, sweat
into each other's body because
it is Chinese New Year and I'm filling
my trays with candies, peanuts, kana,
sweets, embers, hard, nothing;
and I am looking
for the reddest red, the sweetest meats,
the loudest firecrackers and the hardest
plum blossoms to help me make
another year.

Refuging

I.
Where is my refuge,
my fine and feathered friend?
Sitting in the blue glow
of the steam room
where men pass each other
like ghosts, silent;
suspicious, surveying
and strapped for some
humanness, I look through
the billowing wisps
of vapor to the man
standing at the door.
His strong limbs, all
I ever knew how to lean on,
His broad brown body, all
the touch I ever remember;
How often I have wanted him,
to feel his warm spit
against mine,
and to smell his fleshy need.
And if I never saw his face
again, I will know I last saw it,
handsome as ever,
passport size in the back pages of a newspaper.
And while I chase his shadow
down dimly lit hallways
with sticky floors
and sounds of other men
finding their bits of godsend,
I find that I do not show
up in a mirror anymore.
I have become yet another ghost,
like Caspar, friendly
and unselective.

Where is my refuge,
my fine and feathered friend?

In the smoke of the woodfire oven,
the smells of roast pork and chicken,
the chipping of ice blocks,
the popping of Anchor beer for the adults,
Pepsi for the kids,
and the clacking of mah jong tiles,
I watch my family at reunion.
Uncles and aunts prying into
each other's children
secretly comparing notes.

Where is my refuge, my fine
and feathery friend?
Hiding in the space
in which I loved you,
and the body
in which I find you,
demands it.

Where
is my refuge, my fine,
and festive friend,
from the roles of filial
concern inbred
through centuries
of parent and child
cycles of the necessity of home?
And while I hear the static of long
distance phone calls and air letters,
all caught between come and stay;
but homes and familial comforts
hold nothing in this court
of duty, shame
and responsibility.

Where is my refuge,
my worn and weary friend,
from the men who loved me,
from the myths and philosophies
thrust upon me and my race?
Where is my refuge from the belief

that I will live to a hundred and five
that I will never get cancer,
nor high blood pressure
nor heart disease?
Where is my refuge from the men
who say, "I don't really like Asians
but they're so much safer to fuck
these days"?

Where
is my refuge,
my fine, my feathery,
my worn, my weary friend?

II.
When his lover fell,
he carried his man, his brother,
his life on his back
and dashed out into the foggy
rancid early morning freeze;
but the 5 a.m. cabs would not stop
because two Asian men
unsure on their legs
one draped over the other's shoulder
lifeless and shivering, both
looking pissed drunk and frantic
look like trouble,
you never know which gangs you'll fall foul of
this side of Chinatown
if you pick them up.

Falling into the E.R. of St. Marks
he comes face to face,
with the clerk, moonly white,
glowing Jesuslike
in his standard issue hospital gown, who says
"You have to take him to St. Luke's
we don't speak your language here,"
and he shuts the window
in a silent movement of the hand,
quiet and final
as the two men whose combined weights equaled

not the balance of language,
the difference,
nor the truth of any matter,
slouch into the Dettoled floor,
silent, angry,
and dying.

III.
Touch the ground.
Feel the stubble of the newly grown
crab grass creeping across the earth,
damp from December rains.
This is the feel of a man I once loved.
Kneeling on the ground,
the wetness seeps through my jeans
marking two wet spots.
I wish I had flowers,
some marigolds, carnations and irises,
to put on the ground to break the monotony
of wet soil and another Human Services burial.
What's the use of sobbing over a metal plant label,
so washed out you can't even read the name,
much less the date of birth or the date
it all ended?

Sometimes, I call your number
knowing that it has been disconnected
for months. I want the reassurance
of the recorded message telling me that.
Often, I slam the receiver down after the second ring,
heart pounding, afraid
that someone might actually answer.
No one will. Silence
invents a belief that holds solidly
to memories. The feel of your body,
its sweat-salt taste, the musty smell
of cigarette smoke in your hair,
all silenced, replaced.

Nowadays, people I don't know call
to tell me how sorry they are.
Bill calls and says it was a nice funeral.

I meet him later in the bar,
vodka-tonic in his hand,
he saunters over to tell me
I really shouldn't be alone
at a time like this.
"I'll drive you home," he says,
and I remember his absence
on the end of the line
when I called him
after you called me
to tell me you were halfway
dying. Not that he wasn't there,
he just didn't want to speak to me
in the presence of his boyfriend
because that would be tricky.
So I went to the supermarket
because I did not want to be alone
and that did not help,
so I ran as far as I could.
Across the ocean, all the way
to New Orleans. There,
drunk half-assed out of my mind,
I wished you were with me
when I fucked the Belizian dope dealer
while his sister slept
in the same room behind a screen.

Walking in some nameless graveyard
at 3 a.m., feeling the wet grass
on my soles, feeling unpinned down
and invisible,
I came back.
Cleared the board.
Started life from GO.
I've been around the board
so many times, I've lost count
and you in the process.
But I'm here now.
And I know where you are.

IV.
Where is my refuge,
my wise and worldly friend?
Where is it?

V.
Continuing Miss Saigon,
    "Tonight the heat is on."
The first boats fresh
from fire in the Gulf
descend on Pataya, Bangkok
for some R&R. The men have all been given
rubbers and watched safe sex videos
before being let loose on the
available and waiting brown boys and girls
patient for their American G.I. dreams
of hard dicks and U.S. dollars,
and any one from this batch
of seventy thousand odd
can bring hope
of Hollywood movie romance:

> Mel Gibson meets innocent native
> boy, falls in love with his pure
> virgin fuck and after being shipped away,
> comes swimming back across the ocean
> to bring him across the Pacific to live
> in the splendor of Rodeo Drive,
> Fifth Avenue and American Express.

While over at the Rome Club,
the boys, prancing on stage
like a buffet for the Europeans
with big hearts and bigger wallets,
— though everyone knows a few dollars
goes a long way here —
are wearing their
Don't be silly - Put a condom on your willy
t-shirts, courtesy of some American foundation.
As they gyrate and touch their slim bodies
in front of appreciative sex tour loads,

dreaming of love and economics,
none asks what the shirt says,
nor do the few who do speak English
have an idea what a willy is;
these are costumes assigned
by the Boss Man, and whatever gets
the customers is what works,
but the white woman smiling self-satisfied
at the side of the stage can now go home
and sleep safe and happy
knowing that she saved
some third world natives
from themselves,
as each of them disappears,
as the night drags on,
into the back room
or, if they're really lucky,
into the warm Hilton or Sheraton
where maybe even breakfast awaits them,
as they disappear
as the nights drag on.

VI.
Some days, just leave.
Just pack it all up.
Let them tow away your car.
Let the plants die.
Let the cat run away.
Let your shiny white bicycle rust away.
Some days, just go.
Leave it all behind.
Death is the only way out,
now that alcohol has failed
and AA meetings are meaningless
as coffee and doughnuts.
The appetite is gone.
Don't have any urges
anymore, except maybe
to start again.
But you can't do that.
The half life of this body

is short. Nothing
is immune, anymore.
The banquet table is spread.
Pick at the food,
maybe it'll feed
this dying body
struggling to find a life, a way out
of the pain of knowing
living can never be the same,
not when you have the terminal bug.
Sometimes, you just got to
kiss it all away, let go,
once and for all,
lie back, and maybe wait
for the peace to come
or not.

VII.
Where is my refuge,
my wonderful and wintry friend?
Where do I find it?

VIII.
When a voice finally speaks
across the void of stillness,
how many of us will be gone,
how many will I have left,
committed to picture memories
and the mind feel of touch
against my body?
Fingerprints ingrained to my flesh
and smells that hit me
when I let my guard down
during silence, the meniscus
of nothingness
that cannot be broken.
Not even by the passionate fist punching
air shouts of "Silence = Death."
Nor the falseness of a Queer Nation,
the lie of Brotherhood,
or the bigger lie of "G.W.M. G.B.M. G.L.M. G.A.M."

Decibels mean nothing playing
in the numbers racket.
Palm up, odds
slimmer than the lottery
cut across the whole U.S. of A.
What makes you say
"Pick a number
and I will prove you wrong"?
Existing in numbers that don't measure up
and comforting ourselves
in this belief, waiting
for the quiet to fall dead around some ankles
before anyone even notices.

I try to be fearless.
I try to be numb
and always
I'm back where I started.
And everyday a new refuge is lost.
My grief cannot turn angels to gods,
nor can it tear demons from men.
All it does is hold me down, quiet,
to nights when nothing speaks
and nothing is light
as mildew lifting.

IX.
Where is my refuge?
Give me refuge,
O watchful,
O warrant friend.